THE ART OF THE
WANDJINA

I. M. CRAWFORD

Curator of Anthropology and Archaeology at the Western Australian Museum

THE ART OF THE
WANDJINA

Aboriginal Cave Paintings in Kimberley, Western Australia

Published in association with the Western Australian Museum

Melbourne

OXFORD UNIVERSITY PRESS

London   Wellington   New York

Oxford University Press, Ely House, London, W.1

GLASGOW NEW YORK TORONTO MELBOURNE WELLINGTON
CAPE TOWN SALISBURY IBADAN NAIROBI LUSAKA ADDIS ABABA
BOMBAY CALCUTTA MADRAS KARACHI LAHORE DACCA
KUALA LUMPUR HONG KONG TOKYO

Oxford University Press, 7 Bowen Crescent, Melbourne

First published 1968

National Library of Australia REGISTRY NUMBER AUS 67-2022

Registered in Australia for transmission by post as a book
PRINTED IN AUSTRALIA BY BROWN PRIOR ANDERSON PTY LTD

Contents

Acknowledgements *page 7*

1 INTRODUCTION 9

2 THE EXPEDITIONS 15

3 PAINTING TECHNIQUES 21
Hand Stencils
Putting on the Paint
Sam's Baler Shell
Cave Paintings at Mamadai

4 WANDJINAS 28
Aboriginal Accounts of the Origin of the
Paintings
The Powers of the Wandjinas
The Behaviour of the Wandjinas
Wandjinas and Rituals

5 WODJIN 38
The Legend of Wodjin
Wanalirri
The Battle Ground at Tunbai

6 DISPERSED WANDJINAS 44
Brockman's Cave
Bundjin-moro
Bunggudmana and the Owl
Morol
Pindjauri
Wadanda

7 THE SEA WANDJINAS 54
The Death of Namarali
The Fish Chase
Changes in Wandjina painting styles
Ship relics at Langgi
Known Intrusions

8 GREY'S PAINTINGS 62
Site 1
The Engraved Head
Site 2

9 THE KAIARA 69
The Bigge Island Figures

10 BRADSHAW FIGURES 81
The Legend of Koion
The Grasshopper Legend

The Importance of the Paintings to the
   Aborigines
State of Preservation
Conclusions

11   OTHER HUMAN FIGURES   91
   The Kakadja
   Djuari
   Warulu at Djilgu
   Lightning
   The Sturt Creek Engravings

12   ANIMALS IN HUMAN FORM   98
   Kubi and Kalambi
   Yams
   The Crocodile at Lily Pool
   The Bearded Man

13   SNAKES   103
   Ungud
   Child Spirits
   Karn-gi and Daualimbi
   The Rock Python at Gibb River
   Ulu Figures
   The Rock Python at Mount Barnett
   Djilgu

14   OTHER ANIMALS   114
   Sugarbag
   Perulba
   The Manning Creek Crocodile
   Dingoes
   Crocodile at Gibb River
   Lizards at Eagle Point

15   CARVED TREES   126
   Carving a Tree
   The Snake and the Moon
   Snake near Karunjie
   Kangaroo scratches, Karunjie
   Human Figures
   Carved Boab Nuts

16   ROCK ENGRAVINGS   133
   Prudhoe Island
   Carpenters Gap
   Linesman's Creek
   Animals

17   THE FUTURE OF THE PAINTINGS   137
   Causes of Damage
   Methods of Preservation

Select Bibliography   140

Index   142

Acknowledgements

This book could not have been written without the help of a great many people. In carrying out fieldwork, I have been heavily dependent on the co-operation of the Aboriginal guides, who have shown remarkable tolerance when confronted by my ignorance of their customs, and on aid given by the station people and at Missions. But perhaps my greatest debt is to Ray Penrose who took most of the photographs and in so doing cheerfully carried heavy equipment long distances in most trying conditions. Permission to reproduce figure 72 was given by Dr A. Lommel, and figure 69, from UNESCO *Australia-Aboriginal Paintings—Arnhem Land*, Plate VIII, is by courtesy of C. P. Mountford. Dr W. D. L. Ride and the Museum Board made the expeditions possible and Miss Sara Meagher, Miss Vera Ansink and Mr W. Boswell of the Museum staff helped in a great many ways. The production of this work by the Board of the Western Australian Museum was sponsored by a special fund for research and publication on Aboriginal art. Finally I would like to acknowledge the support given by my wife, who except for one occasion had to remain at home when I was away on fieldwork, and who encouraged me in a multitude of ways and made very useful comments on the presentation of this book.

1 Introduction

'What's wrong now—did the flood come over your caves? This place of Morol is a famous place and when my father used to take me all around here, it was shiny looking. That's why I brought these people here. Now it is all dull.

'I don't know what happened to you, but all your spirit has gone out of you. No men or women watch over you, for the people who belong to this place—my aunties, sisters, fathers and grannies—they are all dead now. Only I, that belong to another place, came to visit you, but you were lonely for all those people who died and your spirit has gone away now.'

THIS statement, made to a cave painting by one of my Aboriginal guides, sums up the situation of the old people in relation to their past, for a living culture died in their generation. They have seen the way of the life of their fathers with all its standards, its moral values and its aims overthrown and destroyed in a few years. Many of the people died, some of sickness, some were shot, and some were simply unable to adapt to the new standards. Those who survived live in a changed world and only a few maintain a sentimental attachment for the life of the past: they occasionally visit the sacred centres, sing the rain songs when the monsoon approaches, keep the paintings at the fertility centres fresh and rub ochre on the bones of their fathers. In a few years they too will be dead, leaving behind them descendants who are preoccupied with learning the value of money, and how to handle cattle, to add up numbers, to write letters and to drink—learning, in fact, to take their place in a modern community.

The writing of this book is the fulfilment of a promise made to the old people to record the way of the past, so that later generations of Aborigines may know the reasons and the beliefs behind the paintings and engravings of their forefathers. I want to thank those Aborigines who have spoken freely with me on subjects which I was not qualified to discuss, either because my education has been in the white Australian tradition or because—at least when I commenced these expeditions—I did not have enough grey hairs and was too young: but these subjects were discussed so that I might write this book for the old people.

1 Aboriginal paintings in a cave near Manning Creek

9

I hope that this book may also serve to show my own race something of the culture of the Aborigines, a culture which few ever see. Aborigines are usually not anxious to talk about the past which white people find so quaint or regard as so primitive and they remain silent and uncommunicative. It may come as a great surprise to many to find that even now the tattered old men, often half blind, who sit all day in the ration camps doing nothing, will disappear from time to time, throw off the rags of white civilization and sing for days and nights on end the songs of their dream-time ancestors, the songs made by their fathers, or perhaps the new songs learnt during the last race meeting. This is a side of their life which white people never see. If, through this book, I can show that the culture of the Aborigines had its own unique richness and colour, and that, although very different from our own, it was not dirty and degenerate, then I will have performed a service in bringing a better understanding between Australians of different creeds and race.

My own interest in cave paintings stemmed originally from my training as an archaeologist. When I was a student, I visited in France some of the cave paintings left by men who lived by hunting during the last ice age. I often wondered, as have many others, what inspired those men to paint the walls of the caves with horses and bulls, and how they managed to achieve such striking effects. One guessed that these caves were ritual centres of some kind, because it seemed that no one would trouble to paint them without good reason. But no matter how much one speculated on the motives of the artists, the paintings must always remain mute relics from a bygone age.

Aborigines used to paint the caves and carve animals on the rocks just as did the Palaeolithic hunters in Europe and Africa, but in Australia the situation is different, for some of the artists are still alive, and can explain the significance of the paintings, why they made them and how. By recording the attitudes of the Aborigines towards the paintings, I hoped to forestall the situation in which all that was left of the Aboriginal culture which had created them was the relics. Later, I hope to be able to excavate several of the sites as well.

The attitudes which I recorded varied enormously. Bobby Wabi showed a genuine fear of the spirit of a painting when he believed that we had upset it, and when

2 Kimberley scene—the King Leopold Ranges from the air

4 A line of human figures,
Ord River Valley

he had dreamt that the spirit was rising from the sea, with
power to drown us all. Sam Woolagoodjah showed pride
in one painting, saying that this was his spirit-place, the
place where his spirit had come from before it was con-
ceived. In contrast to fear and pride was the contempt
shown by all of my guides for the exquisite little Bradshaw figures which were dismissed as 'rubbish paintings'.

I was unable to witness any ceremonies associated with
the paintings, for although there is some evidence that
ceremonies were once performed, they are not performed
now. I did record the songs which the old men can still
sing and, whenever possible, the myths which narrate the
actions of the figures in the paintings. However, soon after
I had started work on this project, Howard Coate, a
linguist from the Australian Institute of Aboriginal Studies, started making word for word translations of the
same myths, and as his translations will no doubt be
published shortly, I did not spend much time on this
aspect, but concentrated on covering a wide area and
seeing as many sites as possible. Thus his work and mine
should complement each other.

3 Two women, painted at a
site on the Glenelg River

2 The Expeditions

THE first expedition was a visit to the Ord River valley in
October and November 1962. This area was chosen as the
place to commence work because a large-scale develop-
mental programme had been drawn up and it seemed
very likely that the art would be damaged or destroyed.
The immediate danger seemed to arise from the construc-
tion of dams which would cause flooding over many miles
of country, while in the long run the ensuing build-up of
population seemed to augur little good for the paintings.
These fears proved to have been unnecessary, for very
few paintings exist in the Ord valley, and these are below
the proposed main dam site.

The 1963 expedition was much more adventurous, for
we hired a pearling lugger and sailed along the coast
between Wyndham and Broome. The principal aim was
to try to assess the degree of influence of Indonesian
fishermen on the Aboriginal culture, in particular on
Aboriginal art. We know from existing records that these
Indonesians came mainly from the Southern Celebes,

6 A typical
overnight camp
by the
Glenelg River,
1965

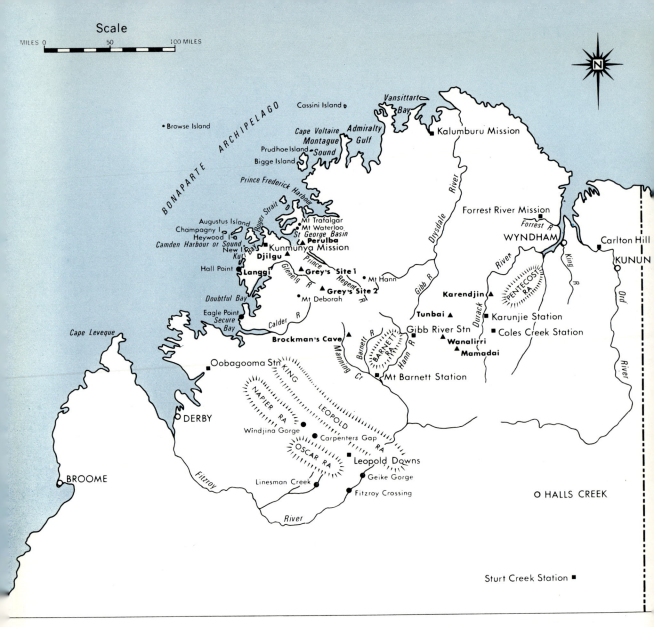

Scale

MILES 0   50   100 MILES

N

• Browse Island

BONAPARTE ARCHIPELAGO

Cassini Island ○

Vansittart Bay

Cape Voltaire
Montague
Sound
Prudhoe Island
Bigge Island

Admiralty Gulf

■ Kalumburu Mission

Prince Frederick Harbour

Augustus Island
Champagny I.
Heywood I ○
Camden Harbour or Sound
New I
Kut
Hall Point ● Langgi
● Djilgu

Roger Strait

Mt Trafalgar
● Mt Waterloo
St George Basin
▲ Perulba
● Kunmunya Mission

Prince
Glenelg R.
Regent R.

▲ Grey's Site 1

● Mt Hann

▲ Grey's Site 2

● Mt Deborah

Dysdale River

Forrest River Mission
Forrest R.

WYNDHAM

King R.

Carlton Hill ■

KUNUN

Ord River

Doubtful Bay

Eagle Point
Secure
Bay

Calder R.

Cape Leveque

DERBY ○

▲ Brockman's Cave

Manning Cr

Barnett R.
BARNETT RA.
Hann R.

■ Karendjin

▲ Tunbai

Gibb R.

Durack River

Gibb River Stn
▲ Wanalirri
▲ Mamadai

PENTECOST RA.

Karunjie Station ■
Coles Creek Station ■

■ Oobagooma Stn

KING

NAPIER RA.

LEOPOLD

■ Mt Barnett Station

Windjina Gorge ●
● Carpenters Gap
OSCAR RA.
RA.
■ Leopold Downs
Linesman Creek ●   ● Geike Gorge
● Fitzroy Crossing

BROOME

Fitzroy

River

O HALLS CREEK

Sturt Creek Station ■

7 Kimberley—the areas visited on the expeditions from 1962 to 1966

8 Human figures, Ord River Valley

16

particularly from Makassar, and that they were searching for trochus shell and bêche-de-mer or sea-slug which they dried and sold to Chinese merchants who, in turn, took it to China. We found two camps with fragments of pottery which we presume was left by Makassarese, as well as three hearths of a type used for smoking bêche-de-mer, but on the whole we could find little evidence that these visitors to the coast had influenced the culture of the Aborigines, and no evidence that they had influenced the art of the area. On this expedition, which lasted for twelve weeks, I was accompanied by photographer Ray Penrose and my wife, and guides from Derby and Kalumburu Mission. These guides were able to show us many art sites in the north-western area of Kimberley.

In 1964 the expedition was a comparatively small-scale venture during which I examined paintings in the Oscar and Napier Ranges in the south of Kimberley and then

worked my way north into Central Kimberley. The purpose of this expedition was to discover how far the typical Kimberley paintings extended to the south and at what point the desert styles replaced them. The Oscar and Napier Ranges contained interesting paintings for as well as those showing influence from north and south, there were paintings of unique local styles, and the area seemed to form a buffer zone with its own peculiarities.

In 1965 I visited sites first recorded by Sir George Grey in 1837 in the Glenelg River area. These paintings have given rise to speculation that foreign people were stranded in Kimberley, and although this speculation died down when Professor Elkin showed in 1930 that similar paintings were produced by Aborigines, and when Howard Coate had taken some black and white photographs of the paintings in 1947, I knew that we could apply modern photographic techniques which would help to show whether these paintings were of Aboriginal origin or not. In order to reach these paintings, we took an aluminium dinghy from Derby as far up the Glenelg River as possible and walked from there to the site. After we had located these paintings, we recorded more paintings in Doubtful Bay and Secure Bay and searched without success for Indonesian relics on islands on the western coast.

The final expedition, in 1966, was an attempt to obtain more information about the paintings in Central and Eastern Kimberley. I had already visited the Central Kimberley area briefly in 1964 and knew that it was extraordinarily rich in paintings, while the area to the east between Gibb River Station and Forrest River Mission was virtually unknown. We were able to travel by Land Rover on this expedition.

Although these expeditions lasted a total of thirty-nine weeks, I am sure that I managed to visit only a small percentage of the total number of sites known to Aborigines. Kimberley is so rugged, and the tracks are so few, that it is almost impossible to penetrate many parts of it. Thus I can present only a sample of the art of the area, although I believe it is a fairly representative sample.

Most of the paintings are in shallow caves, barely more than rock shelters. The overhang of rock provided by the cave is necessary to keep the rain from pouring over the paintings and washing them away. Usually they are not far from water holes, but nor are they close, for then they would be damaged by floods.

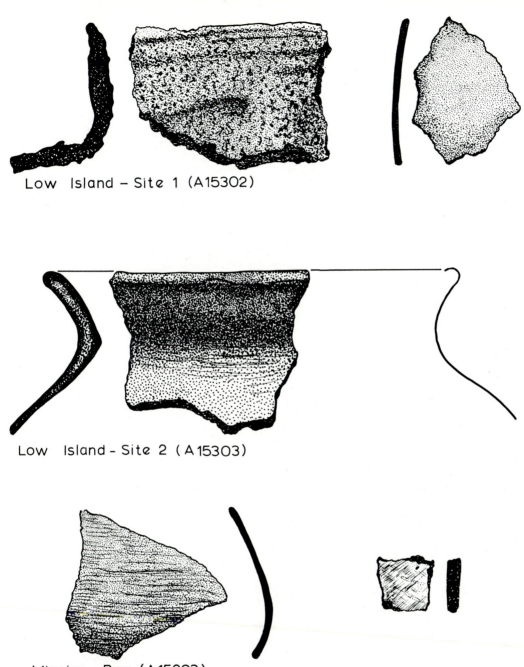

Low Island – Site 1 (A15302)

Low Island – Site 2 (A15303)

Mission Bay (A15293)

RFH.

9 Indonesian pottery found in Kimberley while searching for evidence of outside influences on Aboriginal culture

According to the mythologies, Ancestral Beings, and not the Aborigines, selected these sites for their camps. While these Ancestors occasionally camped in dry places, nine out of ten sites are situated within two miles of a water hole. However, even if one knows that a particular Ancestor camped at a water hole, and that he left a painting behind, it is practically impossible to find the site, for in this rocky country there are thousands of small shelters of which only a few contain paintings. Painting sites are usually marked by upright stones placed in prominent positions nearby, but the untrained eye of the white man seldom notices these signposts.

Nearly all of the sites which I have visited have not been found by chance but have been shown to me by Aborigines who saw the paintings in their youth in the presence of their parents. As many of these Aborigines settled in towns or missions and left the bush between ten and twenty years ago, they experience considerable difficulty in finding their way back to the sites after so many years' absence. The men whose knowledge of the bush, the legends and the sacred places is the most profound are now in their sixties and are generally too feeble or too blind to travel. Men in their late forties and early fifties are less experienced, but are active enough for bush work and it is with these men that I have normally worked. They usually consult the old men as to the location of sites and details of the legends before they leave home. In a few years time the men in their fifties will be inactive and the older men dead and, since younger men are usually ill-informed and the children have never seen the caves and their pictures, it will become extremely difficult to carry out this kind of work in Kimberley.

10 Sam Woolagoodjah translating legends for the author in 1964

3 Painting Techniques

PAINTINGS by preliterate people have been found in many parts of the world, but whereas they are usually relics of dead cultures, in Kimberley the paintings are still of importance to the native people. They still paint pictures using their traditional techniques, techniques which are probably very similar to those once used in other countries. The following descriptions of the ways in which artists in Kimberley have made their paintings may help pre-historians to gain a deeper understanding of paintings in other countries and in other parts of Australia where the Aboriginal cultures have disappeared.

Aborigines in Kimberley voluntarily paint many of the objects which they use in every-day life, for example, carrying-dishes, throwing sticks and didjeridus. I never experienced any difficulty in watching and filming these artistic activities.

However, sacred paintings are another matter. Aborigines are very reluctant to touch the figures painted in caves, for these are very significant in the mythologies. When I was told this, I suggested that a party of men should paint a cave which was of no mythological significance so that they could show me how they made the paintings, and to this proposition three men agreed. One of my guides also volunteered to paint a baler shell for me: he said that these shells had formerly been used on ceremonial occasions, and were therefore painted in the same way as the important paintings. Finally, when I visited one of the principal painting sites in Central Kimberley, my guide expressed disappointment at the dilapidated state of the paintings, and he willingly agreed to the suggestion that he could repaint them.

Thus I was able to observe the painting techniques used by Aborigines on a variety of occasions when objects ranging from those for everyday use to highly sacred ritual items were painted.

HAND STENCILS

The simplest of all Aboriginal paintings are stencils, the shapes left on rock surfaces when an object has had

paint placed around it. Aborigines stencilled boomerangs, spears, even people; but hands were the commonest object.

While I was visiting a site in Secure Bay, my guide, Sam Woolagoodjah, pointed to a small stencil, saying that it was his sister's. He had seen his father hold the girl's hand on the cave wall and spray ochre over it, and he further said that his own stencil, also made by his father, was at another site. When we returned to our base camp, I asked Sam whether he could make a stencil, and he replied that he knew how to make one, but that we were not in his territory and he would not make one in somebody else's country. The stencil, he said, was a mark of ownership, or of belonging to the place, and he had no rights to the camp area. We eventually agreed that if the stencil was made in a place where the tide would wash it away no one would object to his action.

As we had no white ochre with us, Sam used a vegetable dye which he extracted from the branch of a bush. He stripped the bark from this branch, chewed the stem, added a mouthful of water and sprayed the mixture over his hand. When the paint was wet, it was almost invisible, but as it dried, it turned a yellowish-white colour.

Many of the stencils found in Australia show fingers with one or more joints missing and Sam's stencil of his right hand also showed this feature, since he had lost one joint as a child when he had put his finger into a clam-shell which had closed and cut off the end of his finger. It therefore seems probable that stencils with joints missing were not made by bending the fingers over, as has sometimes been suggested, but that they simply show the damage done to the hands of people who lived by hunting and food gathering.

11 Sam stencilling his own hand

12 Aborigines obtaining ochre at Carlton Hill Station

13 An Aboriginal applying dry pigment with his finger

22

PUTTING ON THE PAINT

Aborigines use different techniques to achieve different effects. The simplest pictures are monochrome drawings in which a lump of red or yellow ochre or black charcoal serves as a crayon. No water or binding materials are added to the pigment. Those artists I have seen using this technique have been acting in fun, and the paintings have had no ritual significance or, indeed, much artistic merit.

More complicated figures are painted with two, three or four colours, and for these paintings the pigments are mixed with water and applied as a paint. Once I saw a resin added to this paint in order to give it increased adhesive properties.

In East Kimberley, where I watched paintings being made in two colours, the body of the figure is usually red or yellow and this is surrounded by a series of white dots. White lines and circles are also added to represent the eyes, mouth and navel. The body of the figure may be filled in with ochre, which is used either as a crayon or mixed with water to form a paint. White ochre is always mixed with water. The dots and fine lines are applied with a brush made from a twig, a piece of cane grass or, as is common nowadays, a match stick. If a twig is used, the end is usually chewed to make a kind of fibrous brush.

When three or more colours are used, the painting may be similar in style to the bi-chrome figures, but more usually the artists prepare a white background and apply their coloured ochres over this. The white background is prepared in the following way. The artist finds a flat stone to use as a grinding dish, and on this he rubs the ochre while adding water. When he has obtained a fairly large quantity of paint, he dips in his hand and wipes it over the area to be painted. This preparation covers any water stains, colour variations or any paintings already on the rock surface. The Reverend J. R. B. Love, who was one of the missionaries at Kunmunya Mission on the west coast of Kimberley, reported in his book *Stone Age Bushmen of Today* that it was more usual to spray the white background from the mouth than to apply it by hand.

Over the white background, the red, yellow or black lines of the paintings are applied: thick lines by finger and fine lines by brush.

When the picture of the animal or man has been completed, the artist may add a fine splatter of white paint over it. This he may do by spraying ochre from his mouth, or by taking a handful of wet paint and flicking it over the painting with his fingers.

14 Left: Charlie Numbulmoore applying paint with a brush

15 Below: Sam Woolagoodjah painting dots on the baler shell

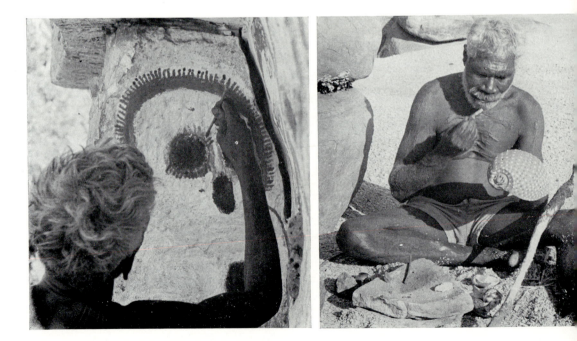

16 Charlie restoring a
painting at Mamadai

SAM'S BALER SHELL

The painting of a baler shell by Sam Woolagoodjah
provided me with an excellent opportunity to observe
some unusual painting techniques.

Sam's first task was to prepare the shell by cleaning all
the slime and algae from its surface, and this he did by
rubbing it in wet coarse sand. He then applied a coating
of red ochre, which he had ground up and mixed with
water and resin. Sam's hand served as an applicator. On
top of the red he applied a series of red and white dots
using a twig brush. Over all this he sprayed yellowish-
white vegetable dye, the same dye he had used to make
the hand stencil. The task took approximately an hour
and a half.

CAVE PAINTINGS AT MAMADAI

When we visited a site called Mamadai, my guide,
Charlie Numbulmoore, stated that the paintings had

seriously disintegrated since his last visit. As he is the only Aboriginal in the area who takes an interest in the paintings these days and is also, through his relations, a custodian of the site, I suggested to him that he should repaint one of the figures. He agreed with this suggestion, which seemed justified since the paintings had obviously been damaged and in their present state were of little value to anyone.

Before Charlie would touch the paintings, he addressed them as follows:

Because you are looking all dull—you're not looking bright— I'll try and draw you. I'll try and put new paint on you people —not my will but because these white people want me to make you new again . . . Don't get wild, don't send rain! . . . You must be very glad that I'm going to make you new— don't try and get wild and don't send the rain to me . . .

These words are recorded here, because they were an action which Charlie felt he had to perform before he could interfere with the paintings, and such a speech was apparently part of the procedure involved in painting figures of mythological importance.

Charlie restored one of the figures by patching up the damaged areas of the painting. He made only minor

18 The black paint was applied
by hand

alterations, being extremely careful to follow the lines of
the previous picture. He first touched up the white background, which had fretted badly, applying the paint with
his fingers, and then repainted the eyes and nose of the
figure, applying a mixture of powdered charcoal and
water in the same way. The third colour in the painting
was red, and, as the red lines were much finer than the
black, Charlie made a brush by chewing the end of a
green stick until it was a mass of fibres, and applied the
paint with this instrument.

Charlie restored one figure completely, and then insisted on adding black to the eyes and noses of the adjoining
figures. The whole task took almost two hours, but it
would have been quicker if we had not interrrupted him
from time to time to take photographs.

When he had finished he once again addressed the
figures:

I made you very good now—I don't know how I did it. Very
good! . . . You must be very glad, because I made your eyes
like new. That eye, you know, like this my eye . . . I made
them new for you people. My eye has life, and your eye
has life too, because I made it new . . .
Don't try to bring rain, my wife might drown with rain. The
rain might drown her . . .

17 Charlie made a brush by
chewing the end of a twig

4 Wandjinas

THE most famous of the Kimberley paintings are the Wandjina figures, huge man-like beings which are sometimes over twenty feet long. These are spectacular paintings, because of their size, and for their colours, as the figures are depicted in black, red or yellow over a white background.

The various physical features of the beings depicted in these paintings usually have two meanings, for the Wandjinas are 'the spirit in the cloud' and the Aborigines understand them to be both human in form and cloud-like. For example, all of the Wandjina figures have an elaborate head-dress which may be described simply as the hair of the Wandjina, but which is also the cloud. The long protruberances issuing from this hair are both the feathers which the Wandjina wore and the lightning which he controls. This dual interpretation is difficult to understand, but it simply means that the cumulo-nimbus clouds which herald the arrival of the monsoon are thought to be the Wandjinas themselves.

Just as the Wandjinas may exist in either human form or cloud, so the paintings of Wandjinas range from human figures to stylized representation of cloud. The sequence from human to cloud form evolves through the following stages: Wandjina paintings usually show man-like figures complete with body, but in some cases the body is omitted and only the head and shoulders retained, and in the next stage the shoulders are omitted leaving just the halo surrounding the face. This is finally simplified until the 'halo' becomes a mass of concentric lines, with only the eyes peering through. Photographer Ray Penrose aptly described this final stage as 'the eye of the storm' (see 20).

The Wandjinas are, then, spirits who are personified as clouds and it is interesting to note that W. Arndt, a senior research officer with C.S.I.R.O., has put forward the theory that the Wandjina paintings have evolved from paintings of cloud. Arndt has watched cloud formations in the Northern Territory and he makes the following points: the clouds often take on a human shape; single clouds move across the sky in an unpredictable fashion

19 Wandjinas are said to be spirits in the clouds. These two are painted at Manning Creek.

28

like a person wandering through the sky. By way of comparison, members of the agricultural establishment at Katherine have frivolously recognized the existence of a being in the sky controlling the clouds and call him Hughie.

Thus Arndt postulates that the Aborigines drew pictures of clouds and later added eyes and noses to these.

Arndt's hypothesis is consistent with statements by Aborigines to the effect that the Wandjinas came out of the clouds and now return in that form: there is no doubt

20 Wandjina paintings illustrating the gradual simplification of style

that the Wandjinas are thought of as beings in the clouds. Arndt's suggestion that the paintings are stylized and humanized versions of cloud paintings is little different from the Aborigines' own statement that the hair and feathers of the Wandjinas are really cloud and lightning.

Nevertheless, there seems to be some evidence to suggest that some of the Wandjinas were human beings of some kind who were intruders in Kimberley. This evidence is discussed later in this book (p. 58) and here it is only necessary to point out that the Wandjinas have power over the rain clouds of Kimberley, and that Arndt has suggested the possibility that the Wandjinas are simply the stylized representation of clouds.

ABORIGINAL ACCOUNTS OF THE ORIGIN OF THE PAINTINGS

The Aborigines state that they did not create the Wandjina paintings, but inherited them from the spirits who first made them. These spirits were the Wandjinas themselves, legendary beings whose activities are recounted in myths and songs. A feature of these myths is that each of the Wandjinas eventually died, leaving his image on the rock where it was painted either by his associates or by himself. The Aborigines used to believe that it was their duty to conserve these paintings by repairing any damage but the original paintings were the creation of the Wandjinas themselves.

The paintings, then, are the illustrations of myths showing the principal characters. These myths are extraordinarily complicated for they tell of the migrations of the various Wandjinas and there are so many of them that almost the whole of Kimberley is criss-crossed by their paths. Their migrations would be impossible to untangle were it not for one event which is included in all, or nearly all, of the Wandjinas' myths. This is the story of the battle at Tunbai between the Wandjinas led by Wodjin and the people (see p. 38). At this point, all of the Wandjinas united, and this event provides a point of reference in the sequence of episodes in the myths, for the events in the myths are said to have taken place before, during or after the battle: in general, the Wandjinas travelled over the country until they were summoned to the battle and after it they resumed their migrations until each reached the place where he was to die and where his painting now remains.

All of the Wandjinas have at least one personal name, and the cave in which each is painted also has a name; for example, the painting of the Wandjina called Morol is at Mamadai. Two at least of the Wandjinas were called Galaru and they have their paintings at sites called Galarungari, one near Mt Deborah, the other near Mt Hann. Because the Galaru are of particular importance mythologically, their name can be used in place of Wandjina, and we had to do this on one expedition because one of our guides objected to the use of the word Wandjina, which had been one of the names of his dead father, and the mention of it could attract the dead man's spirit.

THE POWERS OF THE WANDJINAS

Although the paintings represent the bodies of the dead Wandjinas, the spirits of the Wandjinas live on in much the same way as the Aborigines believe the spirits of human beings continue to exist after their death. These Wandjina spirits have considerable powers and the Aborigines are careful to observe a certain amount of protocol when they approach the paintings, fearing that if they do not, the spirits might take their revenge. This protocol normally consists of calling out to the Wandjinas from several yards distance, to tell them that the party is approaching and will not harm the paintings. In this introductory speech, the Aborigines may justify their visit, saying that their own spirit, or the spirits of close relations came from the site, and that since the last visit the laws of the Aboriginal society have been observed. At the site the spirits must not be upset by frivolous behaviour or, in some areas, by touching the painting.

Should the Wandjinas be offended, the Aborigines believe that they will take their revenge by calling up the lightning to strike the offender dead, or the rain to flood the land and drown the people, or the cyclone with its gales which devastate the country. These are the weapons which the Wandjinas used when they killed the people at Tunbai, and their power to use them remains unabated.

The monsoonal rains which fall in Kimberley between late December and March are believed to be the work of

21 Windjina Gorge, Napier Range
The rock in the middle of the gorge stands in a small pool of water in which baby-spirits are said to be found

the Wandjinas, and the Aborigines sing songs to placate the spirits at these times. The arrival of the monsoon is a dramatic event, and that the Aborigines should assign its creation to supernatural beings is not surprising. This belief may have been reinforced by changes which we observed to take place in one group of paintings: when the humidity rose the ochres become damp and the colours in the paintings become much more vivid, which caused the paintings to stand out more sharply. A similar intensification in the brightness of coloured ochres can be achieved if shiny varnish is put over them, and in some countries it has been common practice to put water on faded paintings in order to make them appear brighter (this practice, however, causes a rapid deterioration in the paintings). In the case mentioned above, the figures in the paintings appeared to be revitalized in the damp conditions.

The Aborigines also believe that the Wandjinas (and certain other beings) control the distribution of the spirits of children. They believe that these little spirits live in water, particularly in the fresh water pools, and that they belong to the Wandjinas. When a man eats fish, turtles or crocodiles taken from the pool, he may consume a child spirit, or it may simply follow him home from the pool.

The man will thereafter dream about the child spirit which is then transferred to the mother. When the child is born, it will be given the name of the Wandjina from whom the baby spirit came.

Wandjinas are not the only beings who control child spirits; some come from the snakes, some from crocodiles, some come down in the lightning and some are the reincarnated spirits of dead people. In eastern Kimberley, the child spirits derive principally from the snakes (see p. 105) but in central and western Kimberley the Wandjinas are the most important source.

The belief held by Kimberley Aborigines on conception was documented by Dr Phyllis Kaberry when she was working in East Kimberley in 1935. She claimed that Aborigines did not know the physical reasons for conception until they were told by white people, and she foretold the situation in which the Aborigines would combine their traditional explanation with the physical reasons. This is the situation now in existence—Aborigines said that they knew that babies resulted from copulation but claimed that this was unimportant, for the spirit of the child still came from, in this case, the Wandjina. We come, they said, not from man, but from the Gods, the Wandjinas:

Our fathers found us in the form of fish or turtles, but the Wandjina is our real father. He put us in the water from the sky. We now call our name from our earthly father, but we came from heaven through the water by dreams . . .

The Wandjinas control the baby spirits not only of human beings but also of animals and so one may find the tracks of infant animals such as emus and kangaroos associated with the paintings of the Wandjinas. Thus the Wandjinas are one of the sources of fertility in the land and the Aborigines believe that if their paintings fall into disrepair, or are defiled, the spirits will leave and the natural species will cease to reproduce.

The terms Wandjina and Galaru are often used by Aborigines to refer to child spirit places. Many of the people trace their spirits back to the Wandjinas and so a question like 'What is that man's Wandjina?' means 'What is the name of the being who inhabited the site from which his child spirit came?'. In some cases, the being is not a Wandjina, but the term is still used. Thus any being which supplies baby spirits may be called Wandjina, although it may be a snake, or a bolt of lightning.

34

THE BEHAVIOUR OF THE WANDJINAS

The behaviour of the Wandjinas provided an example which the Aborigines, on occasions, cited as the correct way to act. This behaviour was, to say the least, socially disruptive. Wandjina legends are full of accounts of the fights between Wandjinas and the people, fights between the Wandjinas themselves, and the stealing of women by Wandjinas from each other.

Aborigines have described the large-scale fights which used to take place between the various tribal groups in Kimberley. They say that these fights were caused by the build-up of grievances, but that the leaders in battle used to incite their men to fight by calling on them to kill as the Wandjinas had done. The stealing of women was also justified on the grounds that the Wandjinas had set this pattern of social behaviour, and that it was not wrong to follow their example.

The Wandjinas may also have introduced certain initiation ceremonies such as circumcision and subincision during their time as wandering beings on earth. According to the legends they certainly practised these rites, but whether they actually introduced them is uncertain. Professor Petri, a German anthropologist, said that when he

22 A Wandjina painted on an upright stone, photographed during the Brockman Expedition in 1901

23 A Wandjina painting on bar
collected by Professor Petri
in 1938

first worked in the area in 1938, the current initiation
laws had come from the eastern side of Kimberley and
were not related to the Wandjinas. It appears that those
initiation rituals, which have now been almost entirely
superseded by desert cults, had also changed in the past,
for Aborigines could recollect an even earlier cult. Thus
it appears that there has been continual replacement of
ritual over a long period, and although the Wandjinas
may have introduced their own version, this has now been
lost.

WANDJINAS AND RITUALS

Apart from witnessing the protocol observed by Aborigines in the presence of the paintings and recording renditions of the rain-songs describing Wandjina activities, I have not seen rituals which derive from Wandjinas. This is not because these do not exist, but because they are not performed any more. Even the songs, as I heard them, were not performed in the traditional manner, for they were accompanied by clicking-sticks, whereas I have been told that in a traditional performance the singer beats a single stick against a baler shell and, at the same time, a clay model of a Wandjina is placed in another baler shell which is full of water, so that, as the songs are sung, the clay turns into mud and the figure disintegrates.

It is known that certain rituals were performed in conjunction with paintings of Wandjinas, but these paintings were not necessarily those in the caves. In 1901 Brockman, the explorer, discovered an upright stone slab on which a Wandjina had been painted, and Professor Petri has collected barks with similar paintings on them. I have been told that such objects were used once only, in ceremonies which included dancing and singing, and after the ceremony had finished, the paintings were abandoned.

Aborigines say that, when the cave paintings were restored, large numbers of men used to congregate and during such an occasion various ceremonies were performed. The custodian of the site, who is one of the men whose child spirit had come from this particular site, had the duty of arranging the meeting and of organizing an adequate supply of food for the occasion. The custodian would not necessarily be chosen to repaint the pictures, for such an honour would be delegated to an individual whose artistic abilities were widely known.

In certain circumstances, food and native tobacco was left at the paintings by Aborigines. At one site was a pile of stones where, according to my guide, young men used to burn tobacco for the Wandjinas while crying out that they had obeyed the laws of their society. On the western coast, there are many fish-traps composed of lines of stones near the high tide mark and these traps are said to have been made by the Wandjinas; for this reason, a part of the catch made in them was left for the Wandjinas.

5 Wodjin

THE legend of Wodjin is the most important of the Wandjina legends for it is the one Wandjina legend which the majority of Aborigines know. After the battle in which Wodjin and his band of Wandjinas slaughtered the people, the other Wandjinas dispersed. Aborigines usually knew this story and the story of those Wandjinas who stayed in their particular part of the country. They had an elementary knowledge of those legends in neighbouring districts, and were usually ignorant of those in distant areas.

THE LEGEND OF WODJIN

The story has many variations, for, being passed on by word of mouth in many different places, modifications were introduced and sections forgotten. Nevertheless, the

24 Tunbai
This photograph was taken at the position from which the Wandjinas attacked the people. The spring mentioned in the story is marked by the large fig tree and dense vegetation in the middle distance.

25 Wodjin was unable to fight and the large rock behind the Aboriginal guide represents him looking over the battle ground

essential facts are always told. Several versions of the story were recorded on these expeditions, but the fullest versions come from people whose child spirits, or whose relation's child spirits, come from the site itself. Their story is as follows:

Two children were playing with the bird Tumbi—they thought it was a honeysucker but it really was the owl. They did not see the difference in the eyes and they thought the bird was not important.

The children maimed the bird, pulling all the feathers from his tail and head, pushing grass through his nose and blinded him. Then they mocked the bird, throwing him into the air, telling him to fly—but he could not and fell back to earth. Then he did fly and disappeared: the boys did not know where he had gone and they did not worry about it.

Now Tumbi was not just an ordinary bird—he was the owl, the son of a Wandjina, and when he disappeared he went up to Inanunga the Wandjina in the sky and to him he complained.

The news flew to the Wandjinas who determined to punish the people. Wodjin called all the Wandjinas throughout the country together, and the bird incited them to revenge.

The Wandjinas assembled their followers—from Munja and from the Calder they came, camping from time to time, fixing their spears for the fight. However, they did not know where to find the people, and the lizards and animals which they sent to scout around for them refused to tell where the people were. The animals were sorry for the people, and tried to hide them, knowing that the Wandjinas would kill them. But Wodjin produced the bicycle lizard from his penis, and the lizard saw the people and beckoned the Wandjinas on.

The Wandjinas saw the people on a wide flat near the

spring at Tunbai. The Wandjinas were on the top of one of the hills which surround this flat.

They then held an initiation ceremony circumcising and subincising themselves, Wodjin saying: 'I want to be light so that I can catch up with those people if they run away.'

Wodjin, however, became ill from this cutting ceremony, swelling up so that he was unable to take further part in the fight. However, he was able to bring heavy rain by stroking his beard, so that the flat was flooded.

The Wandjinas divided into two parties and attacked in a pincer movement from the top of the hill and surrounded the people. Meanwhile the Brolgas had been dancing on the wet ground and had turned it into a bog and the Wandjinas drove the people into the boggy ground where they drowned. The people tried to fight back, but they were unable to harm the Wandjinas and so they were killed.

The two boys who had harmed the bird escaped from the massacre by running away, but when the Wandjinas realized that they were gone, they set off after them. The boys were very frightened by the fight, the rain and lightning, and when they saw a large boab tree with a split in it, they decided to hide inside. But the tree was really a Wandjina and no sooner were the boys inside then it closed on them and crushed them.

The Wandjinas had achieved their aim and revenged the injuries done to the owl. Now they met to decide their future movements. Wodjin moved to a cave, but in the process, he slipped and injured his foot. So he named the cave Wanalirri and decided that he would stay there. The others decided to go to different places, and so the Wandjinas dispersed.

WANALIRRI

The painting of Wodjin can still be seen in the cave at Wanalirri. The cave is really a rock shelter at the bottom of a high cliff in a gorge. On our visit we approached from the opposite cliff, and were able to look down across the gorge and see the cave and the paintings down on the other side. At this point, there is a line of stones to mark the boundary of the sacred ground which we were entering. From our vantage point, one of the guides called out to the paintings, saying that we were bringing hats, shirts, trousers and tobacco, and that we had obeyed the law. As he shouted out, the echo from the opposite cliff seemed to call back to us. When this short speech had been completed, we scrambled down the cliff face, crossed a creek bed which had a little water in it, and went over to the paintings.

The paintings (see 26) are some of the finest Wandjina figures in Kimberley. Wodjin is twenty feet long, with his

26 Wodjin and his followers
at Wanalirri

followers superimposed along his body. Beside his head is
a long branch-like object which is the eatable root of the
native plum tree. Nearby are the animals named in the
legend, the plucked owl and the lizards.

The rock shelter containing the paintings is seventy
yards long, and most of the walls and ceiling are painted.
At the western end, another group of Wandjinas is painted (see 27), the leader of whom was Walamut, and the

ceiling contains frogs and other animals. On the floor of
the shelter is a circle of stones which excited my attention, until I was told that it marked Dr Lommel's camp
fire in 1938!

THE BATTLE GROUND AT TUNBAI

This region is rich in art sites and legends, but there
are also many puzzling problems which arise from the
legends. Were these Wandjinas just mythical beings, or
were the myths a description of some intrusive group?
Several factors seemed to point to the Wandjinas being
intruders—they arrived in an already created landscape
to which they made only the smallest modifications,
people were already on the land, and the Wandjinas
carried on in a very ill-behaved way. These factors dis-
tinguished the Wandjina mythologies from the usual
totemic ancestors in the Aboriginal mythologies.

The logical place to look for any evidence in support
of the theory that the Wandjina legends derive from the
activities of some intrusive group was Wanalirri and the
battle ground at Tunbai, and I was able to visit this area
on two occasions. The chance of finding any material
evidence was remote in the extreme, and all the features
in this area which were pointed out by Aborigines as
relevant to the battle could easily be explained as the
work of either Aborigines or nature. However, there was
one unusual stone arrangement running up the hill over-

looking Tunbai and I spent several hours mapping and examining this site.

Two scars run up the hill, and these are said to be the tracks followed by the Wandjinas in their attack on the people. One of these scars appears to be due to some natural formation, but the other is partly man-made. It consists of two parallel lines of stones which run up the hill to a point where the natural slope is broken by a flat area. Here the lines widen to form a rectangle fourteen feet across. My guide indicated that the lines of stones marked the edges of a track which had been cleared. He said that this track had been in good condition until recent years, but that heavy rains one year had damaged it. In fact, the track had turned into a gully, presumably because the removal of the stones had destroyed the natural surface and permitted erosion to take place. The erosion had been so severe that the gully had cut through the rectangular area into the hill behind and caused a small landslide in the area.

Thus the stone arrangement had been almost destroyed by erosion and landslides, and there was no chance of finding any objects which might have been left by its builders. The only curious feature of the stone arrangement is that it is perched on the slope of the hill, whereas the usual Aboriginal stone arrangement is on a flat area and is used for ritual dances and ceremonies. It is unlikely that the structure at Tunbai was used in this way, for it was difficult to climb up the slope to the enclosed rectangle, and to dance up the track seems impossible. So, although the structure is a curious one, it provides no clues to the question: who were the Wandjinas?

27 Walamut and associated Wandjinas at the western end of the cave at Wanalirri

28 Stone arrangement at Tunbai. The stones line a track running down the hill overlooking the battle ground. The track is that used by the Wandjinas.

43

6 Dispersed Wandjinas

THE Wandjinas described in this chapter are examples of those who dispersed from Central Kimberley after fighting the people at Tunbai, or who were in some way associated with the fight.

Aborigines use the term Wandjina in two ways. Wandjina, they say, is any 'spirit in the clouds'. There are several groups of beings who fit into this definition, but who did not go to Tunbai and fight the people. For example Jumuru and his mother Widjaru travelled to the north along the western coast, the Kaiara came from the northwest to the coast, and Bundulmeri came from Port Keats in Northern Territory to Forrest River. But while the Aborigines use the term Wandjina for these groups, they recognize that they are separate in that their legends have nothing to do with those centred around Tunbai. Thus they also use the word Wandjina in a more restricted sense to mean this inter-related group.

29 Dr House's photograph of Wandjina paintings, taken at Manning Creek in 1901

30 The same paintings in 1964

Most of the Wandjinas who left Wanalirri went to the west, where many of their tracks cross each other on the way towards the coast, some went to the south as far as the Fitzroy River, and some north to Kalumburu near the northern coast. Few, if any, went to the east.

BROCKMAN'S CAVE

In 1901, F. S. Brockman led a survey party through central Kimberley and on this expedition he discovered seven sites with Aboriginal paintings. The first of these was on the Manning Creek where Brockman found a large Wandjina painting, which he described in the following terms: 'The principal figures consist of a group of 12 figures, some being heads and busts nearly life size, each bust having a sailor's knot or pendant falling from the throat.' The 'sailor's knot' is the patch of colour on the chest of the Wandjina; Aborigines say that it is a representation of the breast-bone.

Among Brockman's party was Dr F. M. House, a medical practitioner who was an amateur photographer. Dr

45

House photographed the paintings, but when he developed the glass-plate negatives, he found them to be a failure. House therefore spent the next day retaking the shots, and on this occasion he produced a superb series of photographs, one of which is reproduced in 29.

Dr House's photographs allow us to assess the degree of weathering which has taken place in the intervening sixty years. On the whole, the paintings have remained in fairly good condition, although it is clear that some deterioration has taken place, the worst damage being at the feet of the vertical figures where the paint has fretted or washed away from the rock surface.

The principal figure represents a Wandjina who, after the fight at Tunbai, fought other Wandjinas, was wounded in the leg and subsequently died. His followers painted his picture in the cave and buried him there, and Aborigines have followed this example and placed the bones of their dead in a pile near the paintings. In Brockman's day, bones were plentiful at the site, but now only a few remain and they have been displaced. In 30, two painted skulls which have rolled off the pile of rocks and bones are visible in the cave.

As the Wandjina made his way to the cave, he was followed by ants which made a path lined by stones to the cave and these stones are still in place. Near the cave is a series of circles composed of stones which are said to be the resting places for bodies before they are finally placed in the burial pile. On the ground in front of the cave are rock engravings showing large leaf-like objects which my guide said represented the spear-heads used in the fight between the Wandjinas.

BUNDJIN-MORO

Not many miles away from Brockman's cave is another site which is almost identical with it. The principal Wandjina is again shown lying on his side with his associates painted vertically over his body, although in this case there are eleven followers instead of twelve, and the painting is readily distinguishable from that found by Brockman by the position of the feet of the Wandjina, which are here shown in the middle of the painting, whereas in Brockman's they are near one end.

The two paintings are, however, extraordinarily similar,

46

31 Lines of stones
mark the track of
the Wandjinas and
the pursuing ants

32 Rock engravings
depicting the spear-heads
used in the fight between
the Wandjinas

and in view of the statements made by Aborigines that one man, or a very limited number of men, would be chosen to paint a site, it appears probable that the one artist was responsible for both paintings.

The figure represents a Wandjina called Bundjin-moro, who came to the site after the fight at Tunbai. The cave, according to the legend, was carried from the Calder River in the west by other Wandjinas, who were called to Tunbai before they had had time to paint their own pictures on it. Some of the smaller Wandjinas depicted in the painting are said to be female.

The site is an important centre for child-spirits, both human and animal, and the tracks and pictures of these spirits are represented on the ceiling of the cave. In a nearby cave, various other beings are shown, including evil spirits (Agula) and Wandjinas.

33 Bundjin-moro and his followers, Manning Creek

BUNGGUDMANA AND THE OWL

An interesting group of Wandjinas is shown in 34. In these figures the bands on the bodies and arms have been omitted; but in the horizontal figure, the breast bone is enlarged and the legs have rather more shape than is usual. On the stomach of one of the figures is a bird. The reason for this painting is explained in the following legend recounted by Sam Woolagoodjah.

Two Wandjinas left Tunbai chasing the grey owl for they wanted to keep the bird for themselves. The bird, however, kept flying along just out of reach. The Wandjinas chased the bird all around Kimberley, but they could not quite catch it.

At this place another Wandjina, Bunggudmana, met the bird flying along and he grabbed it. The two Wandjinas, still chasing the bird, came along and met him, saying:
'We are looking for the owl.'
'He's here—but he's mine,' replied Bunggudmana, 'I can't give him back to you.'
'Never mind,' said the Wandjinas, 'You can have the bird. We are very tired and will stay here now.'

The Wandjinas lay down, and they were so tired that they could hardly make the cave and that is why it is such a small one.

MOROL

34 Bunggudmana, the two Wandjinas and the owl, Manning Creek

Morol, a Wandjina, left the Mount Hann area near the Prince Regent River to hunt down the hill kangaroo. The

D

legend recorded here was told by Charlie Numbulmoore and translated by Albert Barunga:

Morol was walking around, and he found the fresh tracks of the kangaroo, and he said to himself: 'Where did he go to?'

Then he got his spear and went after him, and he followed the tracks all the way. That kangaroo looked up the hillside where he had to climb, and he saw the dingoes up at the top of the track.

Morol followed behind to the Durack River, saying 'Where did he go to? He must have gone this way!' and he found a new track and he followed it until he found the kangaroo sitting down. He cornered the kangaroo, calling the place Mamadai, and he put the painting in the cave.

When Charlie saw the paintings, he was distressed at the extent of their deterioration and, as has already been described (page 25), he repainted one of the Wandjina heads. Touching paintings may arouse the spirit of the Wandjina who may send rain and lightning, so Charlie took care to warn the paintings that he was going to repaint them and told them not to be upset by this action which was, after all, for their own good. Despite Charlie's

36 The Wandjina called Pindjauri, who changed into a crocodile, leaving his body at this site in the Oscar Ranges

50

warning, rain followed two days later in the month of the year which is usually the driest month of the dry season! Charlie saw this rain as confirmation of the powers of the Wandjinas and exclaimed: 'Why do these people never believe me!'

PINDJAURI

Some of the Wandjinas travelled to the south at least as far as the Fitzroy River valley. In this area, it is difficult to find well-informed guides; indeed, most of the sites known in this region have been reported by geologists or stockmen, and have been found more or less by chance. I was shown the site of Pindjauri by an Aboriginal, but his information about the legend was rather vague although he was positive that the figure was a Wandjina who came from Galarungari in the north. He left his body in this site in the Oscar Ranges, but his spirit continued 'like a bird' to the edge of the desert where he changed into a fresh-water crocodile.

My guide, who had been converted to Christianity by one of the missions, recounted with glee that an oil drilling company had visited the spring in which this crocodile lived, had captured the crocodile and eaten him.

Neither this legend nor the consumption of the crocodile has been confirmed by other informants, however. Aborigines from more northerly parts said that they did not know this story, but that they were not surprised to hear of Wandjinas so far south since they did know that one other, at least, had come so far.

WADANDA

During expeditions in Kimberley, we twice crossed the track of Wadanda, an adolescent Wandjina whose life, according to the legends, was one series of misfortunes after another.

The story starts at Karendjin on Blackfellow Creek in Central Kimberley. There Wadanda's mother stole and ate the food which he regarded as his own, food which appears to have been the queen ants in the termite hills, considered to be a delicacy by Aborigines. My informant's story runs as follows:

That little boy was playing around here, and his mother hid that Wandjina's food. He thought that it was not eaten but she had some white ants which she left for him. When he came back from playing, he said:
'Mother, where's the food, that meat?'
'Nothing,' she replied.
'No, where's that food that I found here?'

He looked around everywhere, and he broke all the barks while he was looking—he did not find anything, but he broke everything. He tried the white ants, but he threw it away saying:
'That's no good! This is rubbish white ants!'

And he cried, and he cried, but nobody comforted him. So he said:
'This is my homeland—I'll leave you,' and he went down towards the west.

The paintings at Karendjin were almost washed away, but the remains of paint over the walls of the cave suggest that it was once an exceptionally large and important site.

From Karendjin, the boy travelled to the west, and a rock engraving—the only rock engraving of a Wandjina which I have seen—shows his portrait near Mount Barnett Station. At this place, he caught a cold and a stone arrangement nearby is said to represent the mucus which he sneezed on to the ground.

Further west, he had a more fortunate experience, for he met two women who had caught a fresh-water crocodile and some fish, and the three stayed together for a while before Wadanda resumed his travels. During these he was pounding a kind of yam when he hit his testicles, causing them to swell up and drop off. The testicles are said to be at Geike Gorge, where it is said that he has another painting.

37 The rock engraving of Wadanda, near Mount Barnett Station

38 Wadanda and the two women who caught the crocodile, Mount Barnett

7 The Sea Wandjinas

STATEMENTS made in some Aboriginal legends conflict with statements made in others and I have preferred to document these conflicting statements rather than try to reconcile them. In those mythologies which narrate the journeys made by the Wandjinas over large tracts of country and across the territorial boundaries defined by Aboriginal customs, variations exist: for example, in some accounts the Wandjinas came out of the cloud to fight the people at Tunbai, but according to other accounts they were already in the country when they were summoned by Wodjin who sent a hawk as a messenger to them, and they then travelled overland to meet at Tunbai. Whether all of the Wandjinas even went to the fight is also a matter of debate for while some Aborigines say that 'All the Wandjinas went, they couldn't kill the people without the others knowing', these Aborigines do not appear to know any legend which tells how the Wandjinas whose activities are centred on the coast travelled from Tunbai. In contradiction to this statement, one of the old men, Sidie, whose spirit place is on the western seaboard, said: 'Namarali (one of the coastal Wandjinas) is a proper Wandjina, and he comes from Halls Point. He never travelled in to Wanalirri: those people at Galarungari, they moved about, but Namarali stayed in one place.'

In these circumstances, one cannot tell what relationship existed between the Wandjinas in Central Kimberley and those on the coast. The term 'Sea Wandjinas' has, however, been adopted here to distinguish the coastal Wandjinas from the inland groups.

39 The beach at Langgi
The rocks represent Wandjinas
killed in battle

THE DEATH OF NAMARALI

One of the centres for Wandjina activities is at Langgi, a small bay on the western coast. In this area at least two Wandjinas perished, one killed by a stingray, the other speared in a fight. The second legend is of considerable importance to Aborigines, and the version below was recounted by Sam Woolagoodjah and tells of the death

of Namarali (or Daualindi, as he is also called) and his burial on a rock platform.

Namarali was chasing the rock cod, but he could not catch her for she kept slipping through his hands. From this corner to that corner, all around he was chasing her at the place called Langgi. He chased her into the eastern corner when his group met another group of Wandjinas. His people told him:
'They are fighting—they've taken your wife!'
Then he went to the fight and with all the strength he had, he belted the whole lot with his club. He knocked the lot down, but they put a spear into his side then.
The mob looked at him saying:
'Hello—he got speared! He's speared in a fatal place—he will die.'
Everybody cried for him then.

His group carried him away, made the tree platform where his grave is and painted him on the rocks. The people must use the burial platform because the Wandjina used it: that fellow made the law for the dead bodies.

The cave at Langgi where the Wandjina was buried is unusual, consisting of a large slab supported by pillars of rock, and the practice of placing corpses on tree platforms was made in imitation of this rock formation.

An interesting account of the use of these platforms was given by Love, who watched ceremonies during which dead bodies were placed on wooden platforms about six feet above the ground. Around the platform were placed stones, one for each man present. If one of these stones was later found to be contaminated by blood or liquid from the body, the man who was represented by that stone was accused of the murder of the dead man. According to my guide Sam, he had been sent by the old men to examine a decomposed body on one of these platforms. In it he found a glass spear head and from this the old men were able to identify the murderer and they then rubbed blood on the murderer's stone. The burial custom may not, therefore, have been based entirely on superstition but here served in place of an autopsy.

THE FISH CHASE

At Langgi, the Wandjinas had devoted most of their time to catching fish in specially created traps, and several legends tell of the difficulties they experienced in building these. Some fish eluded them, and the Wandjinas gave chase: two rock cod were among those which escaped and the legends tell of their pursuit.

One of these rock cod, described as a black one with a spike on its tail, eluded both the fish trap and the Wandjinas who were tramping around in the water to scare her into the trap. She headed towards the south and swam into Doubtful Bay.

The moon, who was then a man, wanted to kill the fish, and he told the others to chase the fish along to where he was standing. But while he was waiting, a Wandjina called Numbi speared her.

The paintings of the characters in this story are at Doubtful Bay (41, p. 59). They are in a medium sized

56

cave well up in the hills and looking out over the bay and the sea. The view from the site is superb, and one can see islands miles west of the coast. Superimposed over the pictures is a figure painted in the Wandjina style, but whose genital organs are clearly shown, a feature which is unusual in a Wandjina. My guide did not recall seeing this other figure on his previous visit to the site some fifteen years earlier. The paintings which this figure covers resemble the earlier figures at Langgi in style: that is, they too have a large lightning mark running from the halo to the nose.

In the legends, another rock cod, one with a yellow fin, escaped from Langgi and travelled to the north. The Wandjinas made fish traps along the coast in their attempts to capture this fish, but it escaped until cornered in the Prince Regent River.

CHANGES IN WANDJINA PAINTING STYLES

The figure of the Wandjina at Langgi (40) is similar in style to those found elsewhere, but in one respect it is unique for we know precisely when it was painted and who painted it. According to records kept by Love, an Aboriginal painted this figure between January and February 1929. Love made sketches of the figure, and there can be no doubt that it is the one shown here.

One of the interesting features of the Langgi painting is that it is not a restoration of an earlier painting, but a completely new one partly covering earlier paintings. The old men are very secretive about the restoration of paintings, claiming, of course, that the originals are the work of the Wandjinas, not of men. They do admit that these paintings are cleaned and restored occasionally, but it is clear from this example that they sometimes disregarded old paintings altogether.

The new painting at Langgi differs slightly in style from such older paintings as are visible. This allows us to form some idea of the changes in style which have occurred. At Langgi, the earlier Wandjinas have lightning marks running from the halo down across the forehead to the nose. In the later figure, the forehead is not interrupted and the nose is painted as a separate object from the lightning which radiates like hair from the edge of the halo. An almost identical sequence of styles is to be seen

in the paintings at Doubtful Bay which are reproduced
in 41.

We had tried at other sites to discover a sequence of
styles by using infra-red sensitive film. This method,
which is used in art galleries to distinguish paint layers
which have been subsequently covered up, proved of no
use in our studies. Although we could see that earlier
paintings had been covered with white paint at a number
of sites, the infra-red film failed to show us what lay
below the layer of whitewash. Indeed the film seemed to
decrease the contrasts in paint colour which we could
see, for the red pigments were reproduced as a light grey
against a white background whereas ordinary panchro-
matic film reproduced reds as blacks against white.

SHIP RELICS AT LANGGI

It has often been suggested that the Wandjina paintings were first made by, or represented, foreign visitors
(see the chapter on Grey's Paintings for a summary of
these suggestions). Further north, at Bigge Island, we

found positive evidence that foreigners were incorporated into Aboriginal mythologies (see p. 76) and this evidence made it seem feasible that the Sea Wandjinas could have been Aboriginal paintings of sailors of some kind. In the absence of any material evidence to support this suggestion, it was mere conjecture.

In order to look for evidence, I revisited Langgi, where we had previously photographed the paintings. This area was selected as it is an isolated bay in an otherwise inhospitable coast, and one of the few places where a fresh water stream enters the sea. It was also a centre for Wandjina activities and a place where several had died.

Clutching at straws in the wind is usually an unrewarding activity, but sometimes one can be lucky. We revisited Langgi during a spring tide, with a rise and fall of thirty-two feet. At low tide, the bay dried up and we searched it for any form of relic. We found one object, a ballast stone from a ship, near the northern headland, and a little way out to sea there was a dark mass of stones which resembled the ballast of the wreck of the *Calliance* at Camden Harbour. We were unable to wade out to these stones, for a channel separated us from them, and along this channel swam a variety of stingrays and small sharks. Remembering that one of the Wandjinas had died in this same place from a stingray attack, we did not venture into the water.

When we returned to Derby, we asked one of the old men, Sidie, whose spirit place is Langgi, whether there had been any wrecks on the coast. He replied that there had and that years ago someone had retrieved an anchor and chain from it. The survivors, he said, had camped on the northern headland.

I submitted the ballast stone to the Geological Museum in London in the hope that the rock type could be identified and its place of origin discovered. However, the rock is a very ordinary quartzite which might have come from any of a great many countries. The reputed discovery of an anchor and chain suggests that the wreckage was of European or American origin rather than Indonesian.

The discovery of wreckage at Langgi does not prove that the Wandjinas were sailors: all we can say is that there is evidence that foreigners came into the area. Whether the legends recount their activities or not, we do not know, and even if they did, this would not prove that all of the Wandjinas were sailors, for the legends appear to separate those Wandjinas in Central Kimberley from those of the coast.

KNOWN INTRUSIONS

The Kimberley coast has been visited by both Indonesians and Europeans for a long time but the wreck at Langgi is not recorded. The first documented voyage was that of Abel Tasman who, in 1644, with a fleet of three ships, mapped the Australian coast from Cape York to the Abrolhos Islands.

42 The ballast stone found at Langgi—evidence of a shipwreck

43 Informant Sidie

Forty-four years later, Dampier paid a visit to an area identified as Cape Leveque and in one of the nearby bays he careened his ship. Thereafter the coast was deserted until Baudin with his two ships sailed by in 1801 and 1803.

Philip King mapped the coast in 1821. In 1837 both George Grey in the *Lyner* and J. Lort Stokes in the *Beagle* visited the coast, Grey recommending Camden Harbour for a settlement site. As a result of his recommendations, Dr James Martin led a party to Camden Harbour in 1863, and the abortive settlement followed in 1864.

Early in January 1865 the *Calliance*, which had just unloaded settlers and stock, was blown ashore in Camden Harbour at Wreck Point and the remains of the ship (mainly ballast) are visible at low tide. After 1870, pearlers sailed up the coast, but their numbers are thought to have been low since the shell in this area is of poor quality. By the 1890s, when more ships were wrecked, Aborigines in Kimberley had been in contact with Europeans, or had heard of them from the settled areas on the Fitzroy River, and from this date wrecks would have been recognized as such and not treated with any superstition. Thus there is no record which could account for the wreck at Langgi.

Europeans were not the only intruders, for Indonesians also used to visit this coast. We do not know when they first came, although the excavation of their settlement sites may help us to find this out. Baudin's party met a fleet from Makassar on 25 April 1803 at Cassini Island, off the north coast of Kimberley, and a fleet sailed into Camden Harbour in April 1865. The Government Resident of the settlement, H. Sholl, reported that they too claimed to be Makassarese. Visits by people from Timor and the Aru Islands have also been recorded in this area, but little is known about these.

8 Grey's Paintings

In March 1837 George Grey, who was later knighted for
his administration in South Australia, New Zealand and
South Africa, led an expedition into the interior of Kimberley. This expedition was sponsored by the British
Government and the Royal Geographical Society. At this
time, the existence of a large inland sea was postulated,
and Grey set out to discover whether this was the case.
Although he found no inland sea, Grey explored a part
of Kimberley and his report on the physiography and
vegetation led to an attempted settlement at Camden
Harbour in 1864.

While in Kimberley, Grey discovered two sites with
rock paintings of the type which we now call Wandjina
paintings. Grey made sketches of these paintings and
subsequently published them in Volume 1 of his *Expeditions of Discovery* (1841).

These paintings are now recognized as typical of the
Kimberley area, and Brockman (1901), Love (1930),
Elkin (1930, 1948) and members of the Frobenius Expedition (1938) have all recorded many more figures of the
same type. But for many years these were the only figures
known from the area and they aroused a great deal of
interest and speculation, some of the theories being very
fanciful indeed.

SITE 1

Grey visited three art sites, and at the first site he
sketched four paintings. Two of these he described in
some detail, and of the first, a painted head, he wrote
that it:

appeared to stand out from the rock; and I was certainly
rather surprised at the moment that I first saw this gigantic
head and upper part of a body bending over and staring
grimly down at me . . . Its head was encircled by bright red
rays, something like the rays which one sees proceeding from
the sun, when depicted on the sign-board of a public house;
inside of this came a broad stripe of very brilliant red, which

44 The painted head found by
Grey in 1837

45 The four heads seen by Grey,
which he believed represented
women

46 Grey's sketch of the painting shown in 45

47 Grey's sketch of an engraved head, which can not now be found

was coped by lines of white, but both inside and outside of this red space, were narrow stripes of a still deeper red, intended probably to mark its boundaries; the face was painted vividly white, and the eyes black, being however, surrounded by red and yellow lines; the body, hands and arms were outlined in red—the body being curiously painted with stripes and bars.

This painting was revisited by H. Coate and a party in 1947, and we returned to the site in 1965. The painting, which was so bright when Grey saw it well over a hundred years ago, has faded badly. Perhaps it is surprising that it has survived at all.

In the same cave, Grey saw a group of four figures. Grey's conclusion that the four were women, although based on very subjective reasoning, was correct. He wrote:

Upon the rock which formed the left hand wall of this cave . . . was a very singular painting, vividly coloured, representing four heads joined together. From the mild expression of the countenances, I imagined them to represent females . . . each had a very remarkable headdress, coloured with a deep bright blue, and one had a necklace on. Both of the lower figures had a sort of dress, painted with red . . . and one of them had a band around her waist. Each of the four faces was marked by a totally distinct expression of countenance, and although none of them had mouths, two, I thought, were otherwise rather good looking.

48 A fractured rock which could have been mistaken by Grey for an engraved head

64

According to my informant, Sam Woolagoodjah, the four heads represent women, the Mulu mulu, and his story went as follows:

The girls, two mobs, were talking secretly, whispering among themselves: 'What are we going to do with this bloke? Why can't we love him? He's a young man!'

One mob said: 'We will paint ourselves up here and you go on.'

The other mob travelled on, taking the man with them. One girl said: 'I love this bloke! I want him.' But the others replied: 'No! You are making trouble. What are we going to do? We are only women.' They kept on travelling, up to the Prince Regent River. The girl and the man went off then, they had made up their minds.

The single head (44) is said to represent the male Wandjina, while the four heads represent the women who stayed at this site.

If Grey's description of the colours of the paintings was correct, then these figures have also faded in the long period between his visit and ours. Any blue which was once in the headdresses can no longer be recognized, and the colour in 45—a rather murky grey—is very close to the present hue.

THE ENGRAVED HEAD

The cave with the paintings is situated in a rocky ridge which overlooks a flat grassy valley. This ridge continues for about two miles to the west where it is broken by a pass to the south. Between the cave and the pass, Grey found an engraving of a head, which, in his published sketch, looks like the head of a European.

Grey remarked of the head that:

this rock was so hard, that to have removed such a large portion of it with no better tool than a knife and hatchet made of stone, such as the Australian native generally possesses, would have been work of very great labour . . . the ear was rather badly placed, but otherwise the whole of the work was good, and far superior to what a savage race could be supposed capable of executing.

Several hours were spent searching the ridge for this engraving, but in vain. No engraving of a human face could be found, although we did find a natural rock fracture which had a face-like appearance, and which was of those dimensions recorded by Grey.

Grey continued his explorations along the Glenelg River, and near its headwaters he found another cave with paintings. It was his description of one of these paintings, and of the supposed writing over its head, which gave rise to many theories on the origins of these paintings.

Grey wrote:

The principal painting . . . was the figure of a man, . . . clothed from the chin downwards in a red garment, which reached to the wrists and ancles; beyond this red dress the feet and hands protruded, and were badly executed. The face and head of the figure were enveloped in a succession of circular bandages or rollers, or what appeared to be painted to represent such. These were coloured red, yellow and white; and the eyes were the only features represented on the face. Upon the highest bandage or roller, a series of lines were painted in red, but although so regularly done as to indicate that they have some meaning, it was impossible to tell whether they were intended to depict written characters, or some ornament for the head.

Grey was very cautious in his statement about the origins of these paintings, but in a footnote to his account of the expedition published by the Royal Geographical Society, the editor remarked that Grey believed the paintings to be the work of Asiatic people in Kimberley. This suggestion was based on the fact that the paintings showed figures with clothing whereas 'the natives themselves were in a perfect state of nature', and that the paintings were very different from those already seen in Australia. Since the visits by Makassarese to the Kimberley coast had already been documented by Peron and de Freycinet in 1803, the suggestion was not an unreasonable one.

Other scholars were inclined to see other origins for the paintings, and they concentrated their attention on the marks around the head of the last painting and assumed that these marks represented a decipherable script. Thomas Worsnop claimed that the marks were the script from the Red Sea area, and suggested that traders from this area, who were known to have reached Sumatra, might have been carried by storms as far as the Kimberley coast: 'I am a great personage . . .' read the script. J. Panton, interested in the possibilities of contact with Asia, suggested that the paintings depicted Malay or Sumatran figures, the captain having his name on his turban. George

49 Grey's sketch of a painting seen in 1837, which caused much speculation

50 A cave believed to be the one found by Grey near the headwaters of the Glenelg River

Collingridge, famous in his day for his fanciful theories, said that the figures were Moorish and dated from the eleventh century, when the Moors were at the zenith of their maritime power. Professor Campbell, on the other hand, saw the script as Archaic Japanese and translated it as 'the number of the hopeless ones is 62', from which he concluded that a Japanese vessel had been wrecked on the coast leaving sixty-two survivors. Others thought that the marks around the heads represented Hindu turbans, and S. Thornton pointed out that this interpretation was consistent with the shape of the boots worn by the Hindus and shown in the paintings.

All of this speculation was based on Grey's sketches, and therefore could only be valid if these sketches were accurate. Doubt was cast on this point when Brockman photographed Wandjina paintings in which it was clear

51 This figure is believed to be the one sketched by Grey. The photograph was taken through a blue filter in order to increase the contrast in colours.

that the marks in the 'turbans' were not writing. Love and Elkin, both publishing in 1930, then showed that the Wandjina paintings were a part of an Aboriginal religion and that duplicates, if not the original paintings, were being made by the Aborigines. But it was not until 1947, when Coate and a party visited the area and took photographs, that the claim that Grey's painting was Aboriginal could be justified.

The painting which I concluded was that seen by Grey (51) (which is not the same as that seen by Coate) was in poor condition; but this was not surprising since Grey remarked that the painting was already defaced, and 'ancient' in 1837. The halo of the figure has indeed got markings on it, but as far as we could see, these had been created by the weathering away of the paint. This figure had obviously been repainted a number of times, and as the paint on the top layer lifts, it exposes the different pigments used in earlier paintings. This gives rise to a pattern of coloured marks, but as the pattern must change from time to time, it has no significance. We photographed the figure through a variety of filters to increase the colour contrasts, but no writing appeared. The painting appeared to be a typical Wandjina, and there was no indication that it was made by a foreign person.

9 The Kaiara

DURING the 1963 expedition, we visited six sites containing paintings of beings called 'Kaiara'. The Kaiara are very similar to Wandjinas for they also are spirits who are in the clouds and control wind and rain and lightning. They are, like the Wandjinas, progenitors of child spirits, although most of the Aborigines whose spirits came from the Kaiara are now dead. The forms of the figures in the paintings are indistinguishable from Wandjina forms—with a few exceptions which will be described in the following pages.

In the mythologies, however, the Kaiara are quite distinct from the Wandjinas, for the Kaiara came out of the sea from the north and the west bringing, or carried by, the cyclones. They did not travel inland and took no part in the fight between the Wandjinas and the native people. As one guide said:

All these Kaiaras are from the salt water—only the whirlwind was chucking them onto the mainland: the whirlwind was coming bringing the big sea, that's how the Kaiara came to the land . . .

The Kaiara are believed to have very considerable powers over the weather. When a Kaiara is mildly annoyed, he will stir up winds, rain and lightning—as one did when the Aborigines cleared a hornet nest from his face, thereby damaging his paint. On one expedition, when our camp fire spread to the spinifex near another painting, it 'scorched his eyes': the wind and rain which followed in the next twenty-four hours was said to be sent by him in revenge. When a Kaiara is deliberately provoked, he strikes with the cyclone—the water spout which twists around and around over the sea is his penis hanging down from the clouds.

Each Kaiara pursued his own route separately for, unlike the Wandjinas, the Kaiara did not congregate at any one point. Each was accompanied by his children or followers. We crossed four tracks of Kaiaras, each coming from the ocean in the north or west to the mainland or near shore islands.

The first Kaiara site which we visited was Chalangdal

(Chalang-gandalu) on the eastern shore of Vansittart
Bay. The figures painted in the cave are indistinguishable
from Wandjinas. The site is about thirty miles across
country from Kalumburu Mission, and has probably been
visited by Aborigines from the mission who have kept
the paintings in good condition.

The legend tells that the Kaiara were brought to land
from the north by the whirlwind. They landed at Rocky
Cove and spread from there, hiding in the caves, for they,
like the Aborigines, were afraid of the whirlwind. A small
group hid at Chalangdal, and there they remained. Now
they can bring the lightning by blinking their eyes.

Other Kaiara figures were painted at sites further west,
both on the mainland and the islands. The important site

of Wurwai in Admiralty Gulf has been almost washed away, small figures only being preserved in nearby caves.

The main concentration of Kaiara movements appears to have been in Montague Sound and the Bonaparte Archipelago with at least four separate routes coming from the north-west towards the land. At the site of Warabi, a fine example of a Kaiara was painted (56), and in this particular figure, the halo around the head of the figure is greatly extended and represents the cloud which comes with the cyclone. The small figures peeping over the cloud are the children of the Kaiara.

On West Montalivet Island, the Kaiara painting had almost disappeared. This Kaiara came from a reef to the west of the island called Larawai (possibly Albert Reef). He was trying to reach Prudhoe Island, but he became

53 The legends tell that the Kaiara were brought by the whirlwind from the sea. Several sites have been found along the coast of Kimberley.

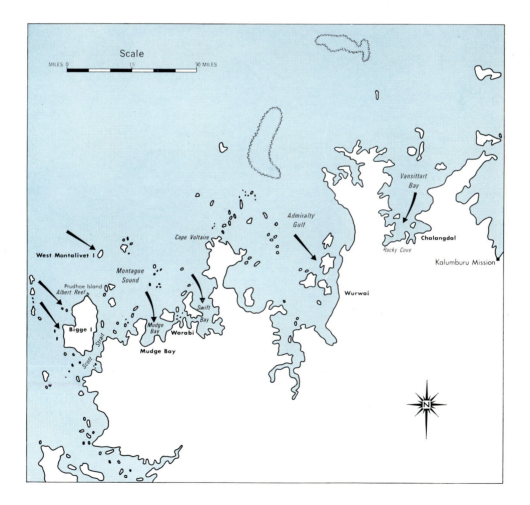

blind and stayed on Montalivet. Also on the island is a large stone arrangement said to have been made by the Kaiara.

Another Kaiara came from the north-west to Mudge Bay. When he approached Kadjingari Island, his catamaran foundered and the Kaiara sank down in the water. All of his children were swimming around looking for their father who walked under the water 'like a diver'. When he came out of the water at Warangala inside Mudge Bay, his children cried for him to welcome him back. While he was under the water, a lot of barnacles had grown on him and the children pulled them off to clean him up. It took a long time, and then they washed him in a fresh-water pool. His painting is on the mainland, and his children are painted nearby.

THE BIGGE ISLAND FIGURES

Undoubtedly the most interesting of the Kaiara figures are those preserved on Bigge Island. At the site which we

54 and 55 Only small figures remain at Wurwai in the Admiralty Gulf

56 The Kaiara at Warabi,
Montague Sound,
with a halo of cloud,
and his children peeping
round it

visited we found one large figure described by our guide
Bobby Wabi as the 'father' Kaiara, and a series of smaller
figures representing his 'children'.

The 'father' Kaiara, (63), is a typical Wandjina type
of painting, but is of course distinct from the Wandjinas
in the mythologies. Particularly striking are his eyes,
which have been engraved in the rock and later painted
black. The lines above the head represent lightning and
cloud. Some of his 'children' are depicted in a similar
style, and one of these is shown in (59), but other figures
are less similar and (60) shows a Kaiara child with a
grossly exaggerated penis which is the water spout.

On our expedition, we were accused of upsetting the
Kaiara, and the following episode is narrated in order to
document the importance of these paintings to the
Aborigines. When we arrived at the site we were immediately warned not to touch the paintings on any
account. We obeyed these instructions, but at lunch time
our fire spread to the nearby spinifex and although we
did our best to keep the heat of the fire away from the
painting, we were warned that we had scorched the eyes
of the Kaiara and he might be expected to retaliate. 'That

bloke, he doesn't waste time', we were told by Bobby, 'he might send the wind and turn the lugger over'.

We had anticipated staying near this site for several days and I had hoped to conduct an excavation; but during the afternoon the wind became stronger and the sky cloudy. That night Bobby saw in a dream two Kaiara coming out of the sea bringing with them the whirlwind. He insisted that we leave the area, convinced that the Kaiara would kill us all. In the ensuing debate, some of the Aborigines maintained that the weather was not un-usual for the season of the year, but traditionally-oriented Aborigines stressed the need to leave the area since they believed that Bobby's dream would come true. We left immediately.

The Kaiara 'children' are represented in a number of paintings, some of which resemble the 'father' while others are rather different. One panel, shown in 64, illust-rates a group of children who, according to the traditions, went into the nearby fresh water where they played with the pythons and emerged eating lily-roots and carrying berries. These items are depicted in the painting, but

58 The principal Kaiara at Chalangdal. These figures are indistinguishable from Wandjinas.

57 One of the Kaiara in the cave at Chalangdal

there can be little doubt that the so called lily-roots are pipes and the berries are water containers.

Nearby is another painting showing three of the children, once again with 'lily-roots' in their mouths, sitting in a boat which is propelled by the central figure who is rowing (61). This method of propulsion suggests that the group was European.

Almost obliterated by sand is another painting (62) which in this case illustrates a sailing ship. The hull is depicted in black, and inside are two more 'children', also eating 'lily-roots'. The ship has two masts and triangular sails.

The paintings at Bigge Island appear to record the

59 A Kaiara 'child' on Bigge Island, the site of many interesting paintings

landing of a party of European sailors but it is difficult to identify this group. The earliest explorer in the area was the Dutch navigator Abel Tasman who mapped the Kimberley coast in 1644. Tasman's log of this voyage has been lost, and we do not know where he landed, but his map is intact, and on it Tasman marked a number of islands along the coast including an island which, if not Bigge Island, is at least situated in the vicinity.

We know that Tasman commanded a fleet of three ships, two of which were yachts with rectangular sails, while the third was a galiot with two masts and gaff rig. The galiot was a small sailing vessel designed for use in shallow waters and this is the ship which one would ex-

60 A Kaiara who represents the water spout

61 and 62 Two most unusual paintings—Kaiara children in a rowing boat (above) and in a sailing-ship (below)

77

pect Tasman to have used for his close shore survey. Interesting features of galiots were the lee-boards which were attached to the side of the vessel and the Bigge Island ship has a circle on the hull in a position which coincides with that of a lee-board on a galiot. Aboriginal paintings were not so accurate that this feature provides proof of identification, but the painting on Bigge Island is not unlike the galiot *Braq* which Tasman used in this vicinity in 1644.

The next documented voyage was two centuries later when, in 1801 and 1803, the Baudin expedition sailed by, but the ships kept well out to sea (to the disgust of the scientists on board). In 1818 Captain Philip King surveyed Bigge Island and sailed through Scott Strait which

63 The 'father' Kaiara on Bigge Island. His eyes have been engraved into the rock and then painted.

78

separates the island from the mainland, but it is unlikely that the painting represents his ship, for he was using a cutter which had only one mast. The painting may represent a pearling lugger, but this also seems improbable for, by the time the pearlers visited the coast, Aborigines would have been familiar with the Europeans and their activities.

It is a matter of some relevance that there is evidence of European wreckage on the Western Kimberley coast which cannot be accounted for in the surviving documentary evidence. The wreckage at Langgi (see p. 60) is one such discovery, but on New Island we also found material which included heavy brass pipes, pieces of iron together with broken china ware and a part of a compass ring. J. Lort Stokes, when exploring the coast in 1837, reported the discovery of a small wreck in Roger Strait. This evidence suggests that the Kimberley coast was visited by many more voyagers than existing documents relate.

Members of the staff at the National Maritime Museum at Greenwich suggested that the rowlocks shown on the rowing boat were of a type used in the nineteenth century and later, but not earlier. At the Scheepvaart Museum in Amsterdam it was suggested that it was improbable that the pipes shown in the sailors' mouths were of the early Dutch type. Thus there is some evidence that the paintings show ships of the nineteenth century. There are references in the available literature which record that American whaling ships visited the north-west coast during the 1840s, and the British privateers who were active in the East Indies may have retreated to the Australian coasts for repairs.

64 The legends say that these children on Bigge Island are eating lily roots

Although it is not possible to identify the group represented in the Bigge Island paintings, there can be little doubt that those visitors were European. This is important, for it shows that the visit of foreigners provided a basis, on one occasion at least, for an Aboriginal legend. Do the other Kaiara legends also describe visits by foreigners to the coast?

The Kaiara legends all tell of the arrival of beings frcm the sea to the north and north-west, usually during bad weather. People could only travel from this direction by ship, and if the legends have any kind of factual basis, then they describe visits to the coast by unknown people. Some of the activities undertaken by the Kaiara suggest that this is the case. How are we to interpret the legend of the de-barnacling of the Kaiara? Ships gather barnacles, and wooden ships had to be careened fairly regularly, but it is difficult to imagine any other object which needs careening. Both Dampier and King found the Kimberley coast a convenient place to carry out this task, although neither careened their ships in the area named in the legend.

The discovery of wreckage at Langgi and New Island, together with Stokes' description of an unknown wreck in Roger Strait, suggest that the Kimberley coast has been more frequently visited than the documentary evidence relates. This is perhaps less surprising when one remembers that Dampier used the coast as a base for his buccaneering activities, and others may have done the same.

European visitors to the coast of Australia regarded the Aborigines as a treacherous race and usually tried to avoid contact with them by frightening them away. Explorers usually fired shots to scare the Aborigines, a procedure which was quite effective, but sometimes they used more unorthodox tactics. Dampier scared the Aborigines by beating his drum and Stokes fired a flare rocket one night with a similar result.

We do not know, and may never find out, how the Aborigines explained the noises and flashes of light produced by the foreigners. For the most part, they had little opportunity to gain close contact or to see how these effects were produced. But thunder and lightning were phenomena they knew, and they may well have explained the activities of the Europeans in these terms and thus seen the intruders as supernatural beings.

10 Bradshaw Figures

65 A Bradshaw figure at Mount Elizabeth Station

ALTHOUGH the Wandjina paintings are impressive because of their massiveness, size and their colour, they lack finesse and movement. In complete contrast are the 'Bradshaw' figures, small red paintings which show people busy dancing and hunting. They have been executed with an eye to detail, for the dress of the dancers—the bangles, the waist tassels and the elongated headdresses—and the weapons of the hunters are carefully depicted. The sense of movement in some of the pictures is extraordinary and the German anthropologists, Dr Lommel and Mrs Schulz, have aptly referred to the style of these figures as the 'elegant style'.

The paintings are usually very small: on an average they measure ten to twelve inches in height but some are less than four inches and others, over twenty-four inches tall, have been found. The paintings are always in red, although the colour varies from a reddish brown to an orange hue.

Mr Joseph Bradshaw, after whom the paintings are called, was an explorer who travelled through Kimberley looking for good pastoral country. He published an account of his adventures together with sketches of some paintings. He commented:

Whenever a profile face is shown the features are those of a most pronounced aquiline type, quite different from those of any natives we encountered. Indeed, looking at some of the groups one might almost think himself viewing the painted walls of an Egyptian temple.

The suggestion that the paintings resemble Egyptian figures need not be treated seriously. However, the little red figures from Southern Africa, illustrated in A. R. Willcox's excellent book, *The Rock Art of South Africa*, are quite similar to those in Kimberley although this similarity does not prove that there was ever any cultural link between Africa and Australia.

Although the Bradshaw figures are often in poor condition or, in some cases, have been painted over, it is possible to recognize scenes in the paintings. For instance, in 66, human and kangaroo tracks, following each other,

F

lead up to the hunter and his quarry and thus form a little scene which tells its own story.

Bradshaw figures are dispersed throughout Kimberley, and although the thickest concentration found on these expeditions was in the north-western area, other research workers say that they are also common in the west. They peter out in the southern regions of Kimberley and are rare in the east.

The paintings closely resemble in style the well known Mimi figures from Northern Territory, and there are similar paintings in northern Queensland. It appears that the paintings in Kimberley are the western-most examples of a style which was once in fashion throughout the northern regions of Australia.

66 This picture at Kalumburu Mission tells the story of a kangaroo hunt

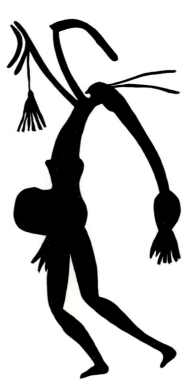

67 A man with a forked spear,
Kalumburu Mission

68 A man holding a boomerang

69 These Mimi figures from Arnhem Land are very similar to the Bradshaw figures

70 Dancing figures, Kalumburu Mission, now badly faded

71 A drawing of the whole scene, with the dancers moving towards singers seated on the ground

THE LEGEND OF KOION

The origin of these paintings presents a mystery. The Aborigines at Kalumburu said that the paintings were not the work of man, but were done by a small bird (*Bramba-bramba*) which lives among the rocks. When the bird sees men or bush spirits, it hits its long curved beak on the rocks until it bleeds, and then paints the pictures with its blood. Sometimes it pulls a feather from its tail to use as a quill. According to another version, the bush spirits (*Koion* or *Djimi*) see the men and spirits and ask the bird to paint the sight for them. Because the bird can see spirits which are invisible to humans, the Aborigines say that they cannot interpret the meanings of the paintings.

71 shows a scene where dancers move towards the singers. Part of this painting is shown in 70, but as much of it is faded and not easily visible, this drawing of the complete scene has been included. Dances in which the performers stamp from one end of a cleared ground towards seated singers were performed throughout Australia.

THE GRASSHOPPER LEGEND

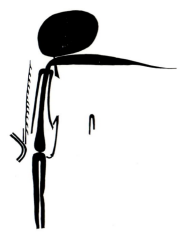

72 This figure, reproduced from Lommel's book, was identified as a grasshopper

In the south-western part of Kimberley, the figures do play a part in one of the legends. This was discovered when I showed to one of my guides a copy of Dr Lommel's book, *Die Kunst des Fünften Erdteils* [The Art of the Fifth Continent], the cover of which shows a Bradshaw figure. He immediately stated that the figure represented the grasshopper which fled from Central Kimberley to the west coast and was caught and eaten by lizards (see page 124). The long thin object with the hooks on it was identified as the back leg of the grasshopper. Although a visit was made later to the area in which the lizards ate the grasshopper, no other Bradshaw figures were identified as representing the insect.

THE IMPORTANCE OF THE PAINTINGS
TO THE ABORIGINES

Unlike the majority of the paintings in Kimberley, the

Bradshaw figures are of no importance to the Aborigines, who simply regard them as the work of a bird. What man, they say, would bother to paint the pictures: such a man would gain no prestige for wasting his time in this way. The paintings are 'rubbish paintings', illustrating nothing of interest or value to the Aborigines.

This attitude is in marked contrast to the respect paid to the Wandjina and the paintings which are associated with myths and songs. It seems probable that the paintings were once of interest but that they are now only relics from an earlier period. Dr Lommel came to the same conclusion from his study of the art of Central Kimberley. The implements depicted with the figures and the poor state of preservation of the paintings offer further support of this idea.

73 A Bradshaw figure at Kalumburu Mission

74 Many Bradshaw figures have been damaged by disintegration of the rock surface

STATE OF PRESERVATION

The Bradshaw figures are poorly preserved and distinct paintings occur only in very sheltered positions. There are plenty of faded and eroded figures, but the discovery of a distinct painting is a rare event.

There are several reasons why the Bradshaw figures are in such poor condition. In the first place many have been partially obliterated by the large Wandjina and animal paintings and no doubt the white backgrounds to these large paintings have covered many Bradshaw figures completely. Very often the Bradshaw figures which have escaped the white-wash are in poorly protected areas of the rock shelters, where the sun has faded them and the rain eroded them. Occasionally even the rock surface on which the paintings have been made has fretted, leaving only sections of the original figures.

Very often, because the figures are dancing or hunting, they hold implements appropriate to those activities. Sometimes the paintings are so clear that one can recognize these implements as identical with specimens in museums. However, in 77, implements from the paintings

75 A line of figures, at Vansittart Bay

76 A Bradshaw figure with spears, found near the Upper Glenelg River

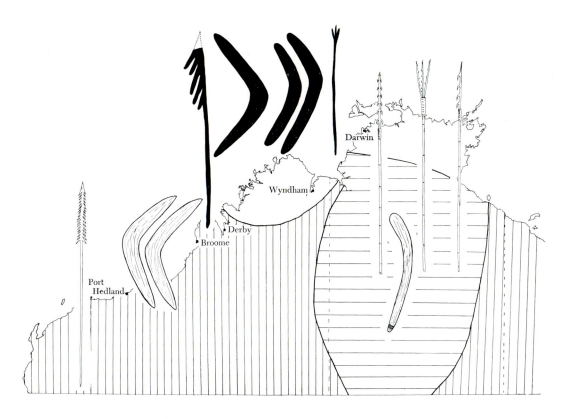

77 Comparison of spears and boomerangs in the Bradshaw paintings (drawn in black) with the existing weapons (in outline), shown in their original locations

are shown beside specimens from Arnhem Land and north-west Australia. The unexpected outcome from this comparison is that the implements in the drawings do not resemble those used recently by the Aborigines in Kimberley. This offers further evidence that the paintings are archaic and represent the artistic achievements of an earlier cultural period in Kimberley.

CONCLUSIONS

The outstanding implement used recently by the Aborigines in Kimberley is a bamboo spear with a stone spear head. The spear head is a leaf-shaped artefact produced by a complicated stone-working technique. Spears of this type are not shown in the paintings and it therefore seems probable that the paintings pre-date the adoption of this spear in Kimberley. The introduction of this spear head is potentially datable by archaeological methods, and such a date might reasonably be regarded as a minimum age for the Bradshaw figures.*

There is good reason to believe that the Bradshaw figures are an archaic art form in Kimberley. The illustration of implements which are not now used in Kimberley suggests that this is the case, and a study of superimpositions, the lack of interest shown by Aborigines and the weathered state in which we find them all support this conclusion.

* It is now known that the stone leaf-shaped spear head has been in use in Kimberley for at least 2480 years. Since this book went to press, a Radiocarbon date has been received of charcoal recovered from an excavation, made by the author at the Pincombe Ranges, Kimberley, in 1962. The dating was done by the laboratory of Professor K. Kigoshi of Gakushuin University, Tokyo, who gave the precise date as 2660 ±90 years before 1950.

78 Dancing figures, Kalumburu Mission

11 Other Human Figures

79 and 80 Evil spirits at
Manning Creek

THE Wandjinas and the Kaiaras are not the only beings
which the Aborigines regard as living and which they
paint on the walls of the caves. The eastern and southern
parts of Kimberley are crossed by the migratory routes of
other beings which are shown in human form, and
throughout Kimberley there are various spirits (mostly
bad) which Aborigines say live in the bush, in the sea,
the rocks or hills. Strange noises at night, and unexplained
marks in the bush, are left by these spirits who are otherwise invisible.

These spirits are usually referred to as Agula (devils),
Djimi (spirits), or Djuari (ghosts). Agula, the devils,
usually inhabit scrub or rocky country. They are roughly
equivalent to the 'bad black man' in our folklore, being
the spirit who will come and take away bad children.
Djimi, the spirits, are apparently less harmful and may
even help Aborigines. Many of the songs which the
Aborigines sing are said to be inspired by the Djimi who
often inhabit caves. Djuari are the ghosts of dead people.
They, and the places which they inhabit, are avoided as
much as possible by Aborigines who evince no desire to
contact the dead.

These spirits are said to be common in certain areas
and to have made certain features of the country such
as hills and rocks. But generally they are not restricted
to any one place and unlike the Wandjinas and totemic
animals, who having reached a certain cave or rock stopped there for ever, many of the spirits can travel over
large areas. They are not restricted to any territorial
limits although, since each can only survive in his own
special environment (sea, rocks, trees etc.), they cannot
go everywhere.

THE KAKADJA

Kakadja is one of the devils who, with his mother
Miminja, preys on children. The following account of
his activities was given by Albert Barunga:

81 Kakadja, the devil who preys on bad children, at Cape Voltaire

Kakadja goes around in the night, and he stands up and waits around to see if any children make noise. He waits for the children and when they cry, Kakadja grabs them. Then he takes them away, up into the mountain and Miminja gets the pounding stone and she pounces on their heads, cracks their heads open and licks their brains out. Kakadja has a penis, a long thing like a rope, and that is what he used to tie the children with and then he would take them to Miminja, his mother.

That is how our mothers used to make us quiet: 'Kakadja might get you!' they used to tell us and we did not cry—we knew about Kakadja. And when any of those children cried, a lot of people would come and stop him. Everybody used to sing out from the camp 'Kakadja might get him!'

Some children used to get very weak, and if they wanted food from anybody, they used to loaf around and would eat anything. They were sick. Well, the people believed that Kakadja had got them.

The painting of Kakadja at Cape Voltaire resembles those of the Wandjinas in style.

82 Djuari, the ghost of a dead person, painted for the author at Wyndham, 1962

DJUARI

Djuari are the ghosts of the dead, and Aborigines consider them to be just as dangerous as Kakadja. All except the very old people may be misled by these ghosts which come back and haunt the burial places. Aborigines have been known to make long detours, especially at night, around those areas in which the bones of the dead have been placed so that they may avoid contact with Djuari.

In the western part of Kimberley, Aborigines believe that the spirit of a dead person makes a long journey after death but eventually returns to the burial place. They say that the spirit leaves the mainland near Halls Point, travels to Augustus Island, Heywood Island and

Champagny Island and finally heads north-west to Browse Island. When it reaches Browse Island, it goes down into the water, but it finds that the water is too cold, so it turns back and returns to the mainland. There is some evidence that Indonesian fishermen used to visit Halls Point, Augustus Island, Champagny Island and Browse Island, and the route followed by the dead spirits may be that once used by Indonesians returning home. If this is the case, it is similar to the situation in parts of Arnhem Land where the mourning ceremonies are a re-enactment of the departure of the Makassarese fleet (see W. L. Warner, *A Black Civilization*).

The bones of the dead are usually wrapped in a bundle with paper-bark and string, and placed in or near the cave from which the child spirit of the man is said to have originated. Thus, when the ghost returns to its bones, it usually returns to the place where it was found as a child spirit. The spirits of the dead may be reincarnated.

On the eastern side of Kimberley, the spirits of the dead take a different route, following the track of Bundulmeri to the east towards Port Keats. They, too, eventually return to the burial site.

WARULU AT DJILGU

Djilgu, a site which is famous for its paintings of Wandjinas and snakes (see page 112), also contains a variety of other human forms. Among these are the Warulu, spirits of the harvest who are depicted with sticks held to their ears. According to Albert Barunga, the Warulu are happy people who live in the rocky areas and spend most of their time dancing and singing. When they defecate they make the yams. Another yam spirit is Ungamin who is shown with a large penis in a rock engraving. The legend tells that the Warulu gathered all of the yams together, but that while they were preparing to dance, Ungamin stole the biggest yams and buried them. When the Warulu discovered this, they tortured Ungamin, pulling his penis so that it is now very long. Ungamin then told the Warulu that if they continued to do this he would not teach them his new corroboree, and so they stopped hurting him and he taught them new songs and dances. He is still in control of the largest yams, while the Warulu have the smaller ones.

94

83 Warulu engravings at Djilgu,
St George Basin.
Warulu are the spirits of
the harvest.

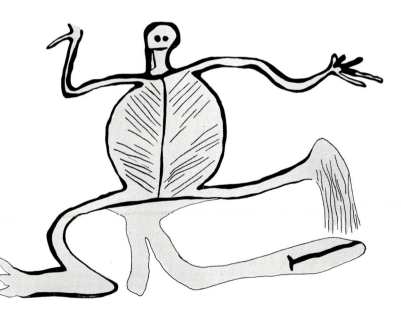

84 Ungamin, who stole the
biggest yams, also engraved
at Djilgu

95

LIGHTNING

Aborigines in Kimberley distinguish two forms of lightning: the 'dry' lightning which precedes the first monsoonal rains by several weeks and the 'wet' lightning which comes with the rain. The first is caused by a being with a separate entity, the second is from the Wandjina and is part of the storm which he controls.

Djandad is one of the names for the 'dry' lightning, and some Aborigines claim that they can call it up at will in order to kill someone or to strike a tree or rock. The lightning may also be called on to help detect murderers. Aborigines believe that the spirit of a murdered man must follow the murderer around: this spirit is normally invisible but it may be detected if one can sleep beside the suspected murderer, for then the spirit will appear during a dream. If the murderer is so wily that he will not allow anyone near him at night, then the lightning bolt must be called up to strike near the man and this will scare the spirit who will be seen to jump away.

Aborigines with the power to call up the lightning may also dismiss it and Dr Lommel recorded that Aborigines at Kunmunya Mission used to chase the lightning, brandishing sticks in order to drive it away.

85 The figure of Djandad, or the lightning, who can be summoned at will, painted at Admiralty Gulf

THE STURT CREEK ENGRAVINGS

One of the most remarkable pictures in Kimberley is a rock engraving at a spring near Sturt Creek Station. This engraving was reported to the Museum by Mrs Blockley, whose husband photographed it during a geological expedition.

The principal figure in the engravings appears to have human form. People to whom the photograph has been shown describe him as 'a knight in armour', and the figure does look like a man wearing a helmet and breast-plate.

One immediately wonders whether this is the work of an Aboriginal, or of some intruder. The style of the engraving does not look Aboriginal, and the technique by which the figure is formed by a series of round pits is unlike any that I have seen. An Aboriginal from the northern part of Kimberley suggested that it could be the work of an 'Afghan' camel driver, for they used to frequent this area.

86 The 'knight in armour',
a remarkable rock engraving at
Sturt Creek Station

However, at the site there are other engravings which appear to merge into the usual Aboriginal styles and techniques. Beside the 'knight' is another engraving which may be a representation of the same figure, but which looks less foreign, and nearby are typical engravings of meandering lines and concentric circles.

My guide from the local station claimed that he had never before seen the engraving, but he did say that according to legend, Djarula, a being who introduced song-cycles and palm trees, passed through the area coming from the south-east, from the Northern Territory. According to Meggitt, an anthropologist who worked in a neighbouring area, Djarula-djarula is the name for a parrot in the Walbiri dialect, and the pattern on the figure may represent the coloured feathers of this parrot.

G

12 Animals in Human Form

MANY of the myths of the Aborigines recount events which took place at a time when man and animal were not clearly distinct. This is the period which we refer to as the 'dream-time' or 'the dreaming', and for which Aborigines in west Kimberley use the term *'lalai'*. At this time the animals, while already possessing most of the physical abilities which they now have, could also change into human form.

In this period are cast many of the stories which tell how certain animals came to have certain features: 'How the scaley-tailed possum got its tail', 'How the porcupine got its spines', 'How the policeman-bird got its red legs' are captions to a few of the hundreds of stories of this kind. They usually commence with the following phrase, 'That fellow [the possum, porcupine or whoever it may be], he was a man that time . . .'.

Sometimes the situation is reversed, so that a story which recounts how an animal came to possess a certain physical feature will conclude by saying that humans got the feature at the same time.

KUBI AND KALAMBI

The most amusing of these stories which I have heard recounts the way in which all animals and man came to possess an anus. Here is Charlie Numbulmoore's account of this story:

Kubi and Kalambi were two herons, Kalambi was white and Kubi brown. And Kubi said: 'What shall I do with this guy— he's too greedy! I never eat any fish—why does he block me all the way? If I had had only one little fish, I would have been alright. What shall I do with this guy?'

And Kalambi's stomach was very large and his legs were very small.

'Well', Kubi said, 'I had better poke him with this kangaroo bone, for he has not got anywhere to let his food out. I haven't got anywhere either, so I might as well poke him and we both will have the same then.'

Then he levelled the ground and he stuck that kangaroo bone inside the ground so that it was sticking out just a little way above the soil. When Kalambi came along, Kubi said: 'Come here, my brother-in-law, come and sit on this good ground which I have cleared for you.' Kalambi sat down then on that bone, and he said: 'What poked me?'

Well the fish came out everywhere, all the types of fishes were all around him and he didn't know what to do. Then the other heron started to get a hole in his behind too . . .

'Never mind', they said, 'We've got something to be proud about. We're alright—we'll go together!'

And the two of them went to the toilet and let their food out every time. That's how that thing came to us, and we people use it too.

With this concept of a basic creation period in which man and animal were not clearly distinct, it is not surprising to find that Aboriginal paintings show animals as humans and beings which combine features of both.

YAMS

Yams consist of a tuber with a crinkled surface and from one end of this tuber extend long thin roots. Aboriginal drawings usually depict the surface of the yam with

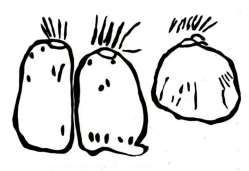

87 The transition from yams to human forms

99

88 Another unusual painting, the 'bearded man' at Doubtful Bay. The man is shown in profile.

89 Crocodile-man painting,
Lily Pool, Leopold Downs

lines or dots, and the roots as long thin lines. These paintings may end up looking like human beings, and figures
in 87 show how easily the transition from plant to human
form takes place. The figures on the left are typical paintings of yams and come from St George Basin, while those
on the right, which come from Kuri Bay, have been modi-
fied so that the roots look like hair, and the protruberances of the yams appear as arms and legs.

THE CROCODILE AT LILY POOL

89 shows a figure which has physical features of both
man and crocodile. This is another example of the trans-
formation from the animal to the human, or *vice versa*,
which takes place so easily in Aboriginal paintings. The
guide was unable to tell us the myths relating to this site.

101

In the Doubtful Bay area we were shown a most un-usual painting which our guide referred to as 'the bearded man'. The man is shown in profile, which is a rare posture, for apart from this painting only a few of the Bradshaw figures are illustrated from this angle. Finally, the figure shows the ribs of the man in a manner faintly reminiscent of the x-ray paintings from Arnhem Land.

According to Sam Woolagoodjah the figure represents Djibida, the tadpole who resembles a Wandjina in having the power to summon cloud and lightning. His mother was a frog who migrated from Gibb River to the western coast. She was already pregnant when she left Gibb River and when the python appeared and the other frogs hid, she took advantage of the situation to escape from them and travel to the west.

The son was born in Western Kimberley and stayed with the mother. When he grew a little, he developed the power to call the cloud and lightning by stretching out his arms.

In areas nearby are paintings which depict frogs in more or less typical fashion, and not far away is a large cave which once contained many Wandjina paintings but these have been almost completely obliterated by water. The 'bearded man' is unlike any of these nearby paintings, and, indeed, it differs from any other paintings in Kim-berley.

13 Snakes

In Kimberley, paintings of snakes are almost as common as Wandjina paintings. The style of painting is similar in that the emphasis is on large simple figures which lack graceful lines. Snakes are predominant among the paintings and mythologies of East Kimberley, but are rarer in West Kimberley. They play almost the same role as the Wandjinas, being associated with the weather, with child spirits and fertility, and they too wandered around Kimberley leaving their portrait in caves, carvings on trees and, occasionally, their infertile eggs as polished rocks in the caves which they visited.

The term most commonly applied to these snakes, or rather pythons, is Ungud. This term appears to be used in much the same way as Wandjina, that is, it means not only the being but also the child spirits which emanate from it and hence may refer to a man's totem. Lu or Lumeri means a snake, and each of the snakes has its own personal name. Capell, the linguist, records that the term 'Galeru' is also used for the snake.

The mythologies relate episodes in the travels of the pythons from the east towards the west. They seem to have passed through the Ord River area, moving then to Forrest River and then south, following or making the rivers. They reached the north-west corner of Kimberley and turned south along the coast, and by the time they had reached Worora country were foreigners using the Wunambal language.

Capell has suggested that the intrusion of the snake mythologies is later than the introduction of the Wandjina cults in Kimberley. This hypothesis is not improbable, and would not be inconsistent with the pattern set by other cults which we know have spread from the south or east. However, at several sites Wandjinas and snakes are closely associated, and at Gibb River the paintings show a single Wandjina in the midst of snake paintings, the Wandjina having helped the snake. This suggests that the two mythological groups were contemporary or have been amalgamated.

90 Paintings of snakes are very common in Kimberley. These were found at Prince Frederick Harbour.

91 Snakes in a cave in East Kimberley

UNGUD

Ungud is the python, also called Lu, Lumeri or Lu-muru. It may appear in several different forms, but it is always connected with water. It may appear as the rainbow in the sky signifying the end of the rain, or as the whirlpool in the sea, or even as a log floating in the water.

Albert Barunga took considerable pains to explain about the Ungud in the water:

When they see the hollow log on the tide, then they used to say: 'Ah! That's the Lu! That's the snake! We can't cross over —it is dangerous. We have seen Lumeri floating by. She's in the whirlpool—we might drown.'

Lumuru . . . well it's like a magic stick: it has got power in it, a snake they used to say. It has only turned itself into a log, but inside it is a snake. It will swallow people.

Those people who tried to cross the Prince Regent, those that sank, well, Lumuru swallowed them—that is what the old people believe. Another lot were lost up at Parry Harbour —they tried to cross the water in a canoe, and they drowned. Lumuru got them! When they see the big log floating in the river which they want to cross, they won't dare go into the water.

CHILD SPIRITS

The snakes provide child spirits in much the same way as the Wandjina: that is, they put the child spirits into the fresh water pools and men may find these either in the form of animals which they have caught in the water, such as crocodiles or turtles, or the spirit may follow the man home. The spirit then appears to the man who informs his wife that he has dreamt of a child. Dr Phyllis Kaberry suggests that in practice the order is reversed: when the woman shows signs of pregnancy, then the man begins to search for the baby spirit and dreams of it.

Many of the paintings at Forrest River are said to represent child spirits associated with Brimera the snake, who created the river itself. In these paintings, the spirits are generally represented as lizard-like creatures with a snout and four legs. In one panel of paintings (92), two spirits are shown superimposed on a horseshoe-shaped design which my guides said was a cave. The spirits, they said, hid in caves and cracks and were generally difficult to find.

Several of the paintings show individuals who were deformed in one way or another. My guides said that children were sometimes born deformed—they recited a long list of deformities such as no foot or a twisted elbow —and said that these deformities were imposed on the child spirit by the fathers during the conception dream. If the spirit appeared in the dream in the form of a crocodile, the father might spear it or break its leg and hence the child would be maimed.

92 Child spirits are strongly associated with snakes. These two, at Forrest River Mission, were apparently hiding in a cave, represented by the horseshoe-shaped design.

KARN-GI AND DAUALIMBI

The figures in 93 represent Karn-gi the moon, and

Daualimbi the black headed python, while the two black figures are ulu drawings (see page 109). The moon and python are the principal actors in a legend which is important as it is the basis for the marriage law in the east-central area. Aborigines observe different marriage laws in different areas, and even within Kimberley there are variations.

Our English kinship terms are inadequate to translate the Aborigines' words for different relations, and my interpreter translated the Aboriginal term Kangai as 'Granny' for the marriage partner, in this case the python, taken in the legend. This may not have been the exact relationship, but it does indicate a prohibited marriage partner.

The legend, recounted by Charlie Numbulmoore, is as follows:

A mob of girls were swimming in the water and Karn-gi, whose name means the moon, sat on the bank. He looked at these girls whom he could legitimately marry and said:
'Oh! They're not too good! They're not fat enough—no tummies!'
But he saw his granny sitting beside them, she was sitting straight on, and he eyed her and said:
'Oh! That's my granny sitting there! Oh dear—what shall I do?
Never mind, I must try and take her for myself.
Cousin, I'll call her, and it is almost straight [legitimate].'
So he grabbed her and took her away from the east to the west, and they lived together. And he loved her because her tummy was fat and so were her legs.
Karn-gi is the man who made up this law, and now the men of this country take women of that relationship for their wives.

THE ROCK PYTHON AT GIBB RIVER

Not many miles away from Gibb River Station is a small cave with a magnificent series of snake paintings (94). The splendid state of preservation and the splashes of paint on the nearby rocks suggested that this site has been repainted in recent years.

According to my informant, Charlie Numbulmoore, the rock python came from the east—we traced its route back to Cole Creek Station and it is said to have come from the east to that point—on a route heading towards the sea. One Wandjina helped the snake and he is shown in

93 Karn-gi the moon and Daualimbi the black-headed python, at Karunjie Station

an attitude which my guide said represented him holding the snake. The snake was travelling with babies, and they are shown in the picture. Sterile eggs are represented by the polished stones which have been placed on one of the ledges. Because the snake was tired and its babies crying, it came to live at this cave. The place is called Mandangari ('belonging to the Manda', which is also a totem for people from that area).

Another informant, Albert Barunga, explained the meaning of Manda:

A long time ago, there was a snake, a rock python, and she had the gum from the Kurrajong tree which is called Manda. She had a lot of gum made into a big ball and she used to

108

94 The rock python and her babies, and the Wandjina who helped her, at Gibb River Station

carry that thing around with her. When she used to kill a young kangaroo or a rock wallaby, she used to wrap that thing in the slimy gum and swallow it down. It was easy to swallow when she put that stuff on. Then people became of that tribe Mandangari—they belong to Manda which is the gum of the Kurrajong and the slime of the snake.

ULU FIGURES

Little figures of people, grotesquely distorted, are often scattered among the paintings of snakes and Wandjinas. These figures are called 'Ulu'.

Ulu is a form of ritual killing, and the figures represent

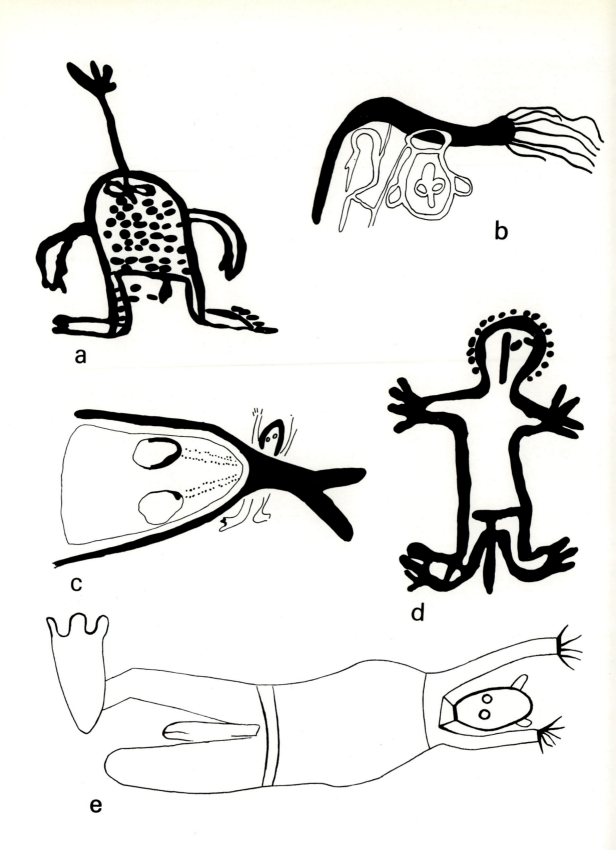

a

b

c

d

e

the victims of this ritual. In order to kill someone, the murderer paints the picture beside the head of the snake, naming the victim and calling on the snake to deal with him. Later on, the victim dreams that the snake has swallowed him, and this arouses in his mind the suspicion that he has been bewitched. The discovery of a new ulu painting confirms this suspicion, and from that point on the man will start to die unless someone has the power to persuade the snake to leave the man alone.

Ulu paintings are sometimes found on isolated rocks or trees because these rocks and trees represent the snake just as fully as the paintings. At the entrance to Windjina Gorge, a large vertical rock represents the snake and, according to one informant, bark paintings used to be pegged to this rock.

Aborigines say that ulu was an effective method for killing in the past, and to judge from the fresh look of some of the paintings, its efficiency has not altogether disappeared. I have had several discussions with Aborigines on the way in which this method of killing worked, and while the traditionally-oriented Aborigines vouch for its infallibility, the detribalized Aborigines point out that it worked perfectly well only so long as the people believed in the powers of the snake or of the 'doctor' who could communicate with the snake. They say that the white people are just as gullible, for they believe in the powers of their own doctors and this belief helps the doctor succeed. In addition there are unconfirmed reports that poisons were also used on occasions to aid the power of the ritual.

THE ROCK PYTHON AT MOUNT BARNETT

The rock python, which had camped at Gibb River, continued on her way towards the west and she travelled along a creek which flows at the foot of the Barnett Range. She camped on this creek, waiting for her egg to hatch, and from it came the Kadbung, her son. But water was scarce at the site, and as it began to dry up, she determined to move on, saying:

'There is no water here, we will keep travelling . . . I am sorry, I should not paint myself, but I stayed here for a long time so I will. Now the country is dry and we will look for good water.'

95 Ulu figures, used in ritual killings, are found in association with snakes and Wandjinas: (a) and (d) are from Vansittart Bay; (b) and (e) from Prince Frederick Harbour; and (c) from St George Basin

111

At the site where she painted herself, rain has almost obliterated the paintings. Only two polished and red ochred stones, her eggs, remained.

The snake travelled on to the west until she reached the Manning Creek which she followed to the north. Near Mt Barnett Station is a magnificent fresh water pool, and when the little snake saw it, he dived in for he was very happy. The mother snake hit the water with her tail, and her son dived in again. Then she stayed there, and painted herself on the cave wall, but she only put half of herself on the rock because she had already left one painting in the range.

DJILGU

Djilgu is a large site about 300 feet above the sea overlooking St George Basin at the mouth of the Prince Regent River. The site is at the base of a vertical cliff

96 The rock python, already painted at Gibb River, ended her travels at Manning Creek

97 A snake and Wandjinas at Djilgu, St George Basin

112

near a trickle of water. The rock shelter contains paintings of a large snake, Wandjina figures and a variety of animals. It is one of the centres for spirits of children.

The legend which Albert Barunga narrated ran as follows:

A mob of snakes, when the snakes were like human beings, were following the rivers. From the Hunter River they came down and they were trying to follow the Prince Regent River. One leader climbed one of the hills to look at the face of the country.

'Oh! That's how the country looks', she said. She followed the river up to Mt Waterloo and Mt Trafalgar. Then she went on to Perulba [see page 118]. She was lying across the rocks, and the bowerbirds were running all around as she lay there. Now you see her as a lot of rocks, but she is still there now, lying in the shape of the snake. Another snake was pounding yams, another was burnt by the bush fire, and another two went right up the Glenelg River where they remained in the water.

This first one was killing all the flying foxes and when she was very full, she looked around: 'Where am I going to lie down and be comfortable?' she said.

So she climbed up the foot of the hill, and lay there. She was so full that she was farting and she said:
'Oh! I must lie down in this place to make camp.' So she lay down, and the place is called Djilgu, the farting place.

14 Other Animals

It has already been pointed out that in the dream-time the present day animals had human forms combined with their animal abilities. Myths, songs and rituals commemorate the activities of these beings, and hills, rivers, trees and stones—the whole countryside—is their creation. There is no feature of the landscape which is not, or rather, was not, explained as the work of these beings: at least, this is the theoretical position, but in fact, since no one person knew all of the legends and many well-versed elders have died in recent years, the mythological explanations for the features in some areas have now been lost.

Aborigines regard these animals as the progenitors of the human race, and each acknowledges a special bond with the particular animal from which he has descended: the animal is his totem and he may have to re-enact the rituals and obey the laws which that animal practised.

There are many variations in these beliefs and in the way in which they influence Aboriginal life: Dr Phyllis Kaberry and Professor A. P. Elkin have both written detailed accounts of the role of totemism in Kimberley and of its variations, and anyone wishing to make a further study of this subject should consult their accounts (see Bibliography).

Kaberry distinguishes four varieties of totemism, of which three have some bearing on the art in Kimberley.

MOIETY TOTEMS. Two birds gave to each other their sisters for wives, and now all of the Kimberley people have one of these birds as a totem and must marry a partner associated with the other. Although we found no paintings of these birds, Aborigines said that the blood of one stained the ground near Carlton Hill Station and thus provided the best red ochre for use in paintings.

98 Each Aborigine acknowledges the animal which is his totem, the origin of his child-spirit, and these are often painted in their spirit places. Such a painting is this one of a lizard, in the Ord River Valley.

99 Barramundi, Ord River Valley

CONCEPTION TOTEMS. When a child is born, it takes its totem from the child-spirit centre of its origin. In western Kimberley the totem may be a Wandjina, but in east Kimberley it is more likely to be a python, while in the south, kangaroos, emus and goannas are more common. Those animals and objects associated with the totem in the myth, are also adopted as minor totems. For example, when one of the Wandjinas lost his axe in a river and, in searching, caught a fresh water turtle, the axe and turtle became minor totems. Many of the paintings depict these animals.

CULT TOTEMS. A few of the animals carried with them sacred objects, such as men's sacred boards and head-dresses, sang the sacred songs and performed the sacred dances. Aborigines still look after these, some being under the guardianship of men, others of women. These ceremonies sometimes include initiation rites.

Nowadays, these cults tend to spread from the south into Kimberley, replacing those which had been previously practised. Thus a young man may be circumcised during a corroboree which had its origins well to the

100 Kangaroo, Ord River Valley

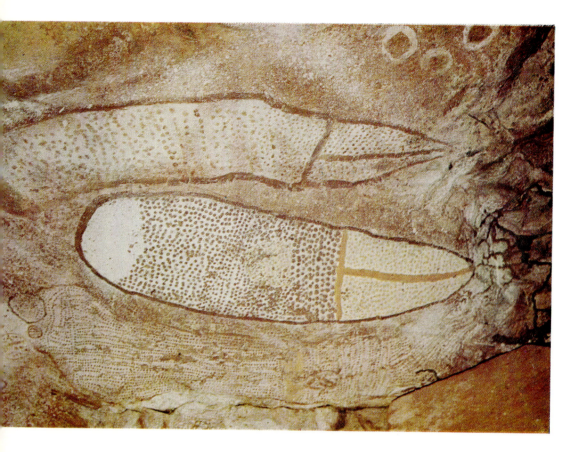

101 Cross-section of a beehive, Secure Bay

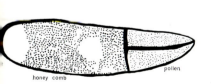

honey comb   pollen

102 The main parts of the hive

south, and should that ritual be the one introduced by, say, the kangaroo, he would be assigned a kangaroo relationship.

SUGARBAG

We visited three sites with paintings said to represent 'sugarbag', the honey made by the native bee.

Aborigines distinguish two varieties of bee, the one which builds its hive in the hollow log of a tree and the one which builds in between rocks in the ground. When they extract the honey from the hive, it is usually mixed up with honey-comb, bees, immature bees and eggs, and the Aborigines put the lot into their mouths—luckily the native bees do not sting—and spit out the inedible parts. A by-product from the hive is the wax from the honey-comb, and this is used for mounting axes.

117

One of the sites with drawings of the hive is in Secure Bay where both the tree-dwelling bee (Waningga) and the rock-dwelling bee (Namri) are depicted. The legend for this site was recounted by Sam Woolagoodjah who said that his step-father who had died about forty years ago had made the paintings.

The two honey bees, Waningga and Namri, were flying along making their 'Worr' noise and a big mob of flies heard them. They were not those ordinary little flies, but big 'dream-time' (*lalai*) flies. The two came on, passing the totem place:
'We will go there, to the lower end of the river,' they said to each other as they came on. The flies were chasing them.
'There they are, those two making the Worr noise!' the flies cried, 'We will have to chase those two'. The two were still searching for a place to make their hives in, but were unable to agree on a place, and all the time those other flies were chasing them. The two would agree on a place, and put their wax on the trees and surrounding rocks and then decide not to stay after all. Two boys who chased them were surrounded by Namri with wax and petrified: they now appear as a black hill in Secure Bay.
Eventually the two agreed on a place saying, 'This is the only place where we can settle'.

PERULBA

From Secure Bay, the bees spread over the country, one of their resting places being Perulba on the Prince Regent River. Of this site, Albert Barunga told the following legend:

The bees separated, different ones went to different places. Some went towards the rock, and others went up the river . . .
Another one was not happy and kept going. He crossed over the Prince Regent and on the other side he found the place called Perulba and there he said:
'I'll try and lie down', and he lay down and was contented.
'Ah. This is the place where I will stay.'
That is the place he remained in, and he became painted on the cave from then until now . . .

As well as the painting of the hive, we found paintings of possums, flying foxes, squirrels (flying possums) and stingrays. Albert explained their presence with this story:

Flying foxes and squirrels were all around that area, feeding when all the flowers were open. They were feeding around, and when they were full, they all came back home. When they were on their way, they found the cave with the bee lying down, so they lay down with him. They joined him.
That stingray is painted there, too, we don't know where it came from: we found it in the cave.

118

103 Another painting of a beehive at Perulba, on the Prince Regent River

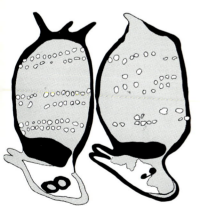

104 Flying foxes

Perulba has served as a burial site, and a number of red painted skulls are just visible on the rocks below the painting in 103.

THE MANNING CREEK CROCODILE

In a small cave on the Manning Creek is a painting of a freshwater crocodile called Unmeleri. The crocodile has a number of circles on the body which represent eggs, and a Wandjina figure nearby.

According to one account, the cuts which the Aborigines used to make on their backs, arms and legs were an imitation of the marks on the skin of the crocodile, but other informants said that they were imitating the brown snake. These marks—tribal marks or cicatrices—were usually made during adolescence and they appear to have been a relatively unimportant stage in the series of initiation ceremonies. The practice has almost, if not completely, died out in Kimberley now.

The legend explaining the origin of the marks on the crocodile was told by Sam Woolagoodjah.

119

105 Flying squirrels

Inonga the crocodile is the fellow who made the law. They asked him:
'Where? Where will we cut the marks?'
'Nowhere', he replied.
'Where? Is this the place?'
'No', he replied.
'What's wrong? Which is the place that you would like—we're asking you?'
'No', he replied.
They kept on asking him, but he would not say.
'We will try a bit further up. Is this the place—between the two shoulders?'
They thought about what they had to do. Then they put the marks on the back of the neck. The crocodile went for his life, he ran away into the water.

106 Sting-ray

DINGOES

A painting showing two dogs was discovered by Dr P. Playford of the Geological Survey while he was examining the Limestone ridges of the Oscar-Napier Ranges. The dogs are in a small cave beside a spring. Billy Munro provided the following outline of the legend, but he was not particularly well informed.

Two dingoes, a male and female, began their travels near Oobagooma Station when they swam across the salt water and crossed the marsh from an island to the mainland. This was a barren area, and they travelled south-east along the ranges until they reached the tableland between the Oscar Napier Ranges and the King Leopolds and the flats to the south at

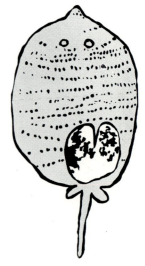

120

107 Unmeleri the crocodile,
in a cave on Manning Creek

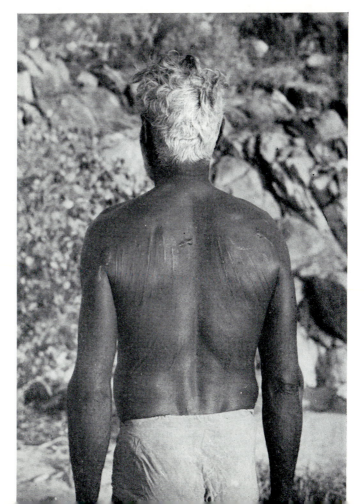

108 Sam Woolagoodjah's tribal
marks

Meda and Kimberley Downs. They travelled through this area, looking for water and scratching holes as they went. They went right down to Fitzroy Crossing, but could find no water. Then a westerly breeze brought them the scent of water. With their noses in the air, they came through Windjina Gorge and went back to the north until they found the spring. Now their paintings show them in the cave, waiting for a kangaroo to pull down as it comes for water.

109 Dingoes, waiting to catch a kangaroo when it comes to drink at the nearby spring, Napier Range

CROCODILE AT GIBB RIVER

A site near Gibb River contains paintings of two fresh water crocodiles and ulu figures. The cave is a very small rock shelter which does not appear to have been inhabited, for there is no smoke blackening on the roof of the

110 Fresh-water crocodiles, who came to hide in this cave at Gibb River Station

cave, no stone waste or ash on the floor.

My guide, Charlie Numbulmoore, approached the cave with more than his usual care, and called out:

We were looking for you all around. Don't get cranky—you must not get wild—you just lie down. We wanted to make sure that we could find you. Truly! Don't get wild—that's not the way—you must be good.

Don't start thinking of rain, the people might be finished. White people were looking for you—it's the same as that Lommel that took your photo here!

Charlie continued with the legend:

Big trouble! They were chasing each other all around the country . . . and they speared him, Wunduk, at Wuliali. And all the children were running this way, and others got killed with stones half way. You, Wunduk, told them to lie down

123

here because you could not take them along. And you looked for a cave to hide in, and when everyone was running away you came to this cave to hide in. It was big trouble! And you hid in this rubbish cave: the others were running away but your knee got too tired, too heavy, and you had to lie down here. And so you are painted on this cave. You called yourself 'Wunduk'.

LIZARDS AT EAGLE POINT

Near Eagle Point on the western coast is a site with a painting showing the top half of a lizard. This was the totem of my guide, Sam Woolagoodjah, and it is interesting to note that he had never been to the site before. He deduced that the painting should be in this area from the information contained in the legend. This legend is also interesting for it contains a reference to paintings of Bradshaw figures, here identified as grasshoppers. The narration was as follows:

The goanna was chasing the grasshopper from Gibb River. The grasshopper hid, but the goanna searched for her and she, frightened, flew on making her noise as she went, 'Debad—debad . . .' The goanna saw her: 'There! There! There!', he called and chased after her, backwards and forwards . . .

All the lizards were painting Mang-got (the lizard) on the rock face when the grasshopper came by. The lizards caught her and hid her. They had got half-way through painting Mang-got when the goanna came and asked:
'Did you people see that grasshopper?'
'Oh—we're a different people to you', replied the lizards.
'Did you see that food? Where did she hide? She may be hiding here somewhere!'
The lizards left the painting, only half the job done, only completed down to the ribs:
'We're another people', they said. 'We never saw the grasshopper coming!'
They were hiding the grasshopper, keeping her for themselves.
'We'll try and find her', said the goanna.
'Try and cook her in the bush oven.'
They cooked her.
'Oh! She's good to eat', they said to the goanna.
'Eat her up! You can eat her—that's alright.'
The lizards ate her, and agreed that they would eat that meat always from that time.

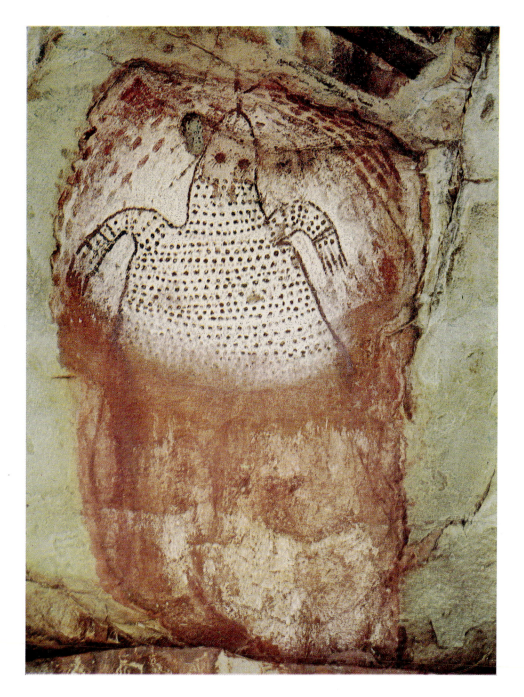

111 The half-completed portrait of the lizard Mang-got, Eagle Point

15 Carved Trees

THE most striking tree in Kimberley is the 'bottle tree' or boab which is closely related to the baobab tree of Africa and Madagascar. The stems of the trees are huge—Philip King measured one with a twenty-nine foot girth—although the trees are not very tall: 'gouty stemmed trees', Grey called them.

The trees provide shade from the sun, and under each tree one can find a slab of stone, which was once used by Aborigines as an anvil on which to break up the nuts of the tree, and a scatter of chips of stone, the waste material from the manufacture of spear heads.

The trees are also convenient reference points used by both Aborigines and Europeans when describing the localities of caves, water holes or rocks. 'It is by the bottle trees', 'Where you see three bottle trees, well, it is near there', are typical expressions which accompany a 'mud map' drawn in the sand.

The stems of these trees are easily marked, and have

112 Boab trees are easy to carve. This devil-ray is at Kunmunya Mission.

113 A carving of a crocodile made at Wyndham in 1962 for the author's benefit

provided a surface for many drawings scratched on with a chip or knife. George Grey was the first to recognize these drawings, although he was not very impressed by them:

I often also found rude drawings scratched upon the trees, but none of these sketches indicated anything but a very ordinary degree of talent, even for a savage . . . .

The main problem which one faces with these carvings is that of establishing who made them, for in this medium, civilized man appears to be in no way superior to the 'savage'. In this era of assimilation, Aborigines usually attempt to carve their names into the trees, although many of them unfortunately twist and reverse the letters —for example, 'RAWKIW'—and occasionally the letters are so disturbed that one wonders whether they were not written in some foreign script. Juxtaposed with these is the contribution of the Europeans who, on the whole, have reverted to cattle brands and primitive stick-figures.

CARVING A TREE

The local Aborigines were questioned about a carved tree found in the Wyndham area. On this occasion, they did not indicate that the trees had any mythological significance, but said they might be found at any of the old camping-sites. They then proceeded to carve a number of trees in and around their own camp.

The technique which they used was quite simple: they used whatever knives were available (principally skinning knives for cattle) and carved their designs into the trees. They then proceeded to fill the excavated areas with paint, applying the usual pigments. The results were quite striking, and a rather drab camp was rapidly turned into an art gallery with snakes, crocodiles and turtles on all of the trees. One Aboriginal, whose camp was under a white-stemmed river gum, did not attempt to carve the tree, but applied the paint over the bark without preparing it in any way.

It is not known whether all of the tree carvings were once painted, but probably some were not. When visiting trees with snakes or long lines carved on them, my guides often picked up a lump of rock and re-scoured the lines in order to make them more obvious but they have never

114 A simple carving of a snake, near Karunjie Station

115 The snake and the moon, who rested here on their travels through the area, and other figures, at Karunjie Station

offered to paint the lines. It therefore seems likely that outlined engravings on the trees were not painted but were frequently re-engraved, whereas the figures with their bodies completely excavated possibly were once coloured although any paint that was on them has now washed away.

THE SNAKE AND THE MOON

One way of establishing whether a carving is Aboriginal or European is to check on its mythological significance: if it is mentioned in the legends, or if it shows an animal which is known to have passed through the area in the dream-time, then it is probably Aboriginal. Such a carving is that shown in 115, for at this site the snake and the moon whose portraits are reproduced in 93 rested. The myth has already been given on page 107.

The principal figure in this carving is a snake which encircles the girth of the huge boab tree. Mixed with the snake is a head and arm, and a mass of lines which cannot now be interpreted.

SNAKE NEAR KARUNJIE

Snakes are a common motif on the trees, and it seems reasonable to presume that these are Aboriginal in origin. They are made up of two horizontal and roughly parallel lines, with vertical lines to represent bands. One of these carvings, shown in 114, is quite near Karunjie Station.

KANGAROO SCRATCHES, KARUNJIE

Another tree near Karunjie is scarred with designs which have no obvious meaning. My guide said that according to the legends, the red kangaroo was travelling through this area, and that the marks were probably made when he was scratching himself.

HUMAN FIGURES

A few of the trees bear carvings of human beings. No explanation was ever offered for these carvings, but in all cases they marked large camping sites and they may represent nothing more than attempts to 'make the place look pretty'.

The first carving that I found was beside the King River near Wyndham; just a little figure lightly carved into the bank of a bottle tree (116). It was probably not very old, and when the present layer of bark flakes away, it will be lost.

116 Carved human figure from Wyndham. The significance of these figures is no longer known.

117 From the Pentacost Ranges

118 From Derby

Another human figure was found in the Pentecost Ranges, about thirty miles west of Wyndham. This figure (117) is more spectacular, for it is wearing a ceremonial headdress. A common headdress in this area is made from paper bark bound with string to form a long conical hat and this may be the kind represented in the picture. The trees in this area were heavily scored, for while few people ever try to cross the Pentecost Ranges those who succeed are inclined to leave their marks. The origin of the figure must, therefore, remain in doubt, although it conforms in style with Aboriginal designs and is not similar to European carvings.

The last human figure to be illustrated here (118) comes from Derby, where boab trees are extremely common. Only one carving which looked Aboriginal was found, although dozens of trees were examined. It is situated in one of the camping areas still frequented by Aborigines who come to Derby during the race season— now glorified as the Boab Festival—and camp under the trees by the edge of the salt marsh.

The figure is not easily recognized as the scar it forms on the tree has almost grown over. It may, therefore, be of some antiquity although the growth rate of these trees appears to be erratic. For example, on Sheep Island in Camden Harbour the grave of Mary Jane Pascoe lies beside a bottle tree on which her name was carved in 1865. The letters are perfectly legible, and it is improbable that they have been renewed; but in other cases, names of explorers have disappeared in much less than one hundred years.

CARVED BOAB NUTS

Not only are the stems of the boab trees carved, but so too are their nuts. These nuts have a dark brown coating which is easily scraped or scratched to reveal a yellow woody layer. Nowdays, Aborigines remove the surface with a penknife blade, often pushing the blade while twisting it from side to side so that a zig-zag line appears.

The nuts do not store well, for they tend to dry out and crack open and as a result old nuts are rare in collections, although new ones are plentiful. At least one Aboriginal has told me that the carving of the nuts is an introduced custom, taught to the Aborigines by Europeans, and because the old nuts are not preserved, it is

difficult to counter this argument; but a few specimens which have been preserved suggest that it is incorrect.

The oldest specimens in the Western Australian Museum differ in two ways from the more recent additions. The old nuts carry designs which are typically Aboriginal —circles and meandering lines are frequent—whereas the modern examples show luggers, animals and dancers depicted in European style. Secondly, the modern nuts have been carved with a steel blade whereas the old ones are more deeply incised by a gouge of some kind. Possibly this was the traditional possum tooth gouge mounted on the end of a stick: such gouges are known to have been used for incising designs on sacred boards.

119 Carved boab nuts.

Top row: left, from Derby; *centre*, location unknown; *right*, Wyndham, 1962—the vertical line represents the road from Wyndham to Kununurra and the adjoining loops are significant places on that road.

Bottom row: left, from Kunmunya Mission, 1948; *centre*, from Derby, but probably done by Sunday Islanders; *right*, from Kunmunya Mission, 1948.

16 Rock Engravings

As well as painting rocks and carving trees Aborigines used to engrave rocks, and representations of animals and human beings are scattered throughout Kimberley. These rock engravings are not common, however, and in this area it is a minor art form, an impoverished display compared with the multitude of figures in the Pilbara one thousand miles to the south. Two outstanding rock engravings in Kimberley, the Wandjina at Mt Barnett and the figure at Sturt Creek, have already been described (see pages 52-3 and 96), and the eyes of the Kaiara were also often engraved.

Although the engravings are few, they were made by a wide variety of techniques: some are cut into the rock, some scratched on the surface, some pounded into the rocks, some have been rubbed in, and the Sturt Creek engravings were possibly produced with some kind of drill. Fragments of white ochre in the grooves of some of the engravings show that they had once been filled with pigments.

On one occasion, when we visited a group of engravings on Prudhoe Island, my guide sat down and immediately rubbed a shell along the grooves which formed the outline of a whale, leaving a powder from the shell as he went. This action, like that of re-cutting the lines in the boab trees, seemed to be designed to clarify the markings; but at the same time this guide remarked that in the old days they went fishing in this area and that they used to clean up the engravings as part of the pre-fishing ritual.

PRUDHOE ISLAND

Prudhoe Island is the only site in Kimberley at which rock engravings are at all numerous and even here less than twenty engravings have been ground and battered into a dark brown rock surface.

The site overlooks an extensive reef which my guide, Bobby Wabi, said had once been a favourite fishing area. When the moon was full a large number of Aborigines

120 Rock engraving, Prudhoe Island

would gather and, after performing rituals designed to ensure success, they would form a line in the water and drive the fish into the shore. A few engravings illustrate fish.

One engraving depicts a woman, identified as Djilinga, a name used for woman or, according to the Reverend Love, for the praying mantis. Bobby sang a song-cycle which told of the adventures of Djilinga and of her desire to return to the northern part of Kimberley. A large foot print was also identified as Djilinga's.

CARPENTERS GAP

In a small cave near Carpenters Gap in the Napier Range is a series of rock engravings and paintings. The rock engravings have been formed by a cutting technique, and consist of two to five inch gashes in the rock surface. Similar gashes appear in many parts of Kimberley, but are usually confined to sandstone rocks and Europeans have suggested that such cuts are formed in the process of sharpening stone implements; although such a process was not witnessed during any of these expeditions, this is not unlikely. When the cuts are arranged in a series of vertical lines, Aborigines have suggested that they were tallies of the number of people who visited the sites.

The interesting feature of the cave near Carpenters Gap is that some of the cuts have been arranged in such a way that they form patterns; in the simplest designs they form bird tracks while the most complicated design is a large crocodile. This example of the transition from purely functional grooves to pictures is similar to the

121 The woman called Djilinga

122 Djilinga's footprint

123 Gashes in the rock develop into meaningful patterns

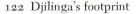

134

124 A crocodile, Napier Range

transitions, described by Strehlow, the anthropologist, from lines and tracks drawn in the sand to sacred designs, which he observed among the Arunda in Central Australia. In other words, simple lines have been converted into designs by a small spark of artistic inspiration.

LINESMAN'S CREEK

In the Pilbara District of Western Australia are many thousands of rock engravings, including a type which we call Gurangara figures. This name was first used by the late Father Worms, a bishop of the north-west, who concluded that this kind of figure was related to ceremonies called Gurangara which were spreading from the desert towards the western coast between the 1930s and 50s. The engravings show men and women with exaggerated genitalia, and the figures are usually very long and thin. Often there is a sense of movement in the engravings, suggesting that the engravings may be a record of ritual occasions.

Similar engravings are rare in Kimberley, although a few human figures have been lightly scratched into rocks in the Ord River and these, like the Gurangara figures, are long and thin and possess large genitalia.

125 Engravings at Linesman's Creek resemble the Gurangura figures of the Pilbara District

135

One cave, situated near Linesman's Creek Range, contains engravings which do bear some resemblance to those in the Pilbara. These engravings are superimposed over paintings of simple red figures, and they appear to consist of a series of human figures joined by lines.

It is interesting that the same Gurangara cult which Father Worms described also spread to Kimberley from the desert. However my guide was unable to explain the function of the engravings, and was not able to discover any evidence that they were associated with Gurangara.

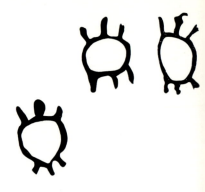

126 Turtles, Ord River Valley

ANIMALS

Animal engravings have been produced by a variety of techniques. The little turtles, 126, have been ground into the rock and, to judge by the fragments of white ochre in the grooves, subsequently painted. The kangaroo from the Ord River, 127, has also been created by this technique but the head of the kangaroo has been battered into the rock surface. The little wallaby, 128, has been entirely battered or pecked into the rock.

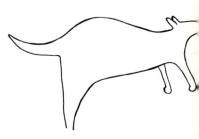

127 A kangaroo, Ord River

128 A wallaby

136

17 The Future
of the Paintings

ABORIGINES used to restore the paintings when they deteriorated, and this method of conserving paintings was maintained until about twenty years ago. A few paintings are still kept in good condition, and occasionally one finds fresh paintings and paint splattered over the adjacent rocks; nevertheless, the majority of the paintings have not been touched for twenty or more years, and they have suffered from the ravages of time.

On many occasions I have been led to sites which, according to my guide, were fresh and clean when they had last visited them and in almost every case the guide has been shocked to discover how poorly the paintings are now preserved. I thought that these guides might have been exaggerating in their statements that the paintings had deteriorated but I was able to see for myself how rapidly paintings disintegrate for in 1966 I visited one of the sites at Forrest River which I had previously seen in 1961. In the interval, a record flood had swept by the paintings, completely obliterating some, seriously damaging others, and it was my turn to say to my companions that the paintings had once been bright but were now destroyed.

The rate of deterioration varies enormously from site to site. The painting at Langgi which was completed in 1929 still looks fresh for it is well protected from wind and rain and, with luck, will remain in good condition for many years. The painting on the Manning Creek which Brockman photographed in 1901 has deteriorated, for the legs of many of the Wandjina followers, which are present in his photograph, have disappeared, although the damage is confined to a small area.

CAUSES OF DAMAGE

The commonest cause of damage is water which, during the 'wet' season, falls very heavily indeed. The rain which falls on the rock is channelled by the rock formations so that it flows across certain areas, leaving others relatively dry, and Aborigines naturally tried to select for their paintings areas which remained dry. But these channels alter from time to time as old ones fill up with leaves or when new cracks develop in the rocks and therefore a painting which was once well protected may be washed away in a few weeks if it happens to be in the way of one of these new watercourses.

Aborigines recognized the need to prevent water crossing painted surfaces and in addition to selecting dry areas they deliberately diverted water by obstructing watercourses with pieces of gum. But this gum only has a short life, and when it falls off the water returns to its former route.

At some sites the paintings are exposed to the sun and they appear to be faded. The effects of light on paints have been examined in art gallery laboratories and it is known that the ultra-violet light emitted by the sun may cause loss of colour. Dust also causes loss of vividness in the colours, for it settles on the paint and cannot be brushed off.

Vandals have so far caused little damage to the paintings in Kimberley. On the whole, the paintings are situated in very remote areas which are not accessible to people with the usual means of transport and thus very few people have been able to see the paintings. In the area near Kununurra on the Ord River, several paintings within easy walking distance of the town have been damaged, being either used as targets for rifle practice and therefore damaged by bullet scars, or added to in a variety of ways, mainly obscene.

Therefore, unless steps are taken to preserve the paintings, they will gradually fade or wash away and perhaps this process of disintegration will be hastened by the thoughtless acts of some visitors.

METHODS OF PRESERVATION

Since the last war, art galleries and museums have become conscious of the problems involved in conserving art objects, and modern museums are in properly designed buildings in which humidity and temperature are controlled for optimum preservation. In these conditions very little deterioration will take place, but in Kimberley, where temperatures vary from freezing point to 127°F in the shade, and where four months of the year are 'wet' and the remainder dry, the problem of conserving the paintings is almost insurmountable.

The problem of conserving rock paintings *in situ* has already been referred to experts overseas. Two methods by which the paintings might be preserved are available, although neither appears to be a very satisfactory answer. The first method is to build some kind of structure, and this is the method which has been recommended by Dr H. J. Plenderleith, the Director of the International Centre for the Study of the Preservation and Restoration of Cultural Property, Rome. At some sites in Kimberley it would be possible to construct shelters which would protect the paintings from wind and rain. But in the more remote areas the difficulties involved in transporting sufficient materials would be very great, though perhaps cement barriers could be constructed to prevent water from cascading over some of the paintings in the same way as the Aborigines used to build gum barriers. This work would not protect the paintings from dust or vandals, but it would prolong their survival.

The second method for preserving the paintings would be to impregnate the paint surfaces with a fixative of some kind. This would convert the ochres into paint with much the same qualities as household paints. However, before we coat the paintings with any chemicals, we need to know much more about the properties of these chemicals. How long will they last? Will they peel off and destroy the paintings? Will they discolour? These and many other questions must be answered before we take a step which could prove abortive, and even destructive.

The situation at the moment is unsatisfactory, for while we know that the paintings are deteriorating, there appears to be little we can do to prevent their eventual disintegration. Until the processes leading to deterioration in the paintings can be halted, the only positive action we can take is to record the paintings photographically and to try and store the photographs under conditions where they will not fade or change colour. This book is an attempt to show the quality of the paintings which will be lost in the years to come, and to tell of the role of the paintings in the culture which created them. That culture, even more certainly than the paintings, will soon be lost.

Select Bibliography

Arndt, W., 'The Australian Evolution of the Wandjina from Rain-clouds', *Oceania*, 1963-4, xxxiv, pp. 161-9.

Basedow, H., *The Australian Aboriginal*, Adelaide, 2nd impression, 1929.

Berndt, R. M., 'Some Methodological Considerations in the Study of Australian Aboriginal Art', *Oceania*, 1958, xxix, pp. 26-43.

Berndt, R. M., (ed.), *Australian Aboriginal Art*, Sydney, 1964.

Bradshaw, J., Notes on a Recent Trip to Prince Regents River, *Transactions of the Royal Geographical Society of Victoria*, 1892, ix, part 2, pp. 90-103.

Brockman, F. S., *Report on Exploration of North-West Kimberley, 1901*, Perth, 1902.

Campbell, J., The Syllabic Characters found on the head gear of a figure . . . found by Sir George Grey . . . *Report* . . . *Australasian Association for the Advancement of Science*, Sydney, 1898, p. 838.

Capell, A., and Elkin, A. P., The Languages of the Kimberley Division, *Oceania*, 1937-8, viii, pp. 216-46.

Coate, H. H. J., 'The Rai and the Third Eye. North-west Australian Beliefs', *Oceania*, 1966, xxxvii, pp. 93-123.

Cranstone, B. A. L., 'The Art, Myth and Symbolism of Arnhem Land', *Man*, 1958, 22.

Crawford, I. M., 'Aboriginal Sites in Western Australia', in Australian Academy of Science, *National Parks and Nature Reserves in Western Australia*, n.d. Western Australia.

Elkin, A. P., 'Rock Paintings of North-west Australia', *Oceania*, 1930-1, 1, pp. 257-79.

Elkin, A. P., 'Totemism in North-western Australia', *Oceania*, 1933, iii-iv.

Elkin, A. P., 'Grey's Northern Kimberley Cave Paintings Refound', *Oceania*, 1948, xix, pp. 1-15.

Grey, G., 'A Brief Outline of the Recent Expedition to the North-west Coast of Australia . . .' *Journal of the Royal Geographical Society*, 1838, viii, p. 454-9.

Grey, G., *Journals of Two Expeditions of Discovery in North-west and Western Australia . . .*, 2 vols, London, 1841, reissued Adelaide, 1964.

Heeres, J. E. (ed), *Abel Janzoon Tasman's Journal of his discovery of Van Diemen's Land and New Zealand in 1642 . . .*, Amsterdam, 1898.

Hernandez, T., 'Myths and Symbols of the Drysdale River Aborigines', *Oceania*, 1961-2, xxxii, p. 113-27.

Kaberry, P. M., 'Spirit Children and Spirit Centres of the North Kimberley Division, West Australia', *Oceania*, 1936, vi, pp. 392-400.

Kaberry, P. M., 'Totemism in East and South Kimberley, North-west Australia', *Oceania*, 1937-8, viii, pp. 263-88.

Kaberry, P. M., *Aboriginal Women—Sacred and Profane*, London, 1939.

Kimberley, W. B., (comp.), *History of West Australia*, Melbourne, 1897.

King, P. P., *Narrative of a Survey of the Inter-tropical and Western Coasts of Australia*, 2 vols, London, 1827.

Lommel, A., 'Notes on the Sexual Behaviour and Initiation, Wunumbal Tribe, North-western Australia,' *Oceania*, 1949, xx, pp. 158-64.

Lommel, A., 'Modern Culture Influences on the Aborigines', *Oceania*, 1950, xxi, pp. 14-24.

Lommel, A., *Die Kunst des Fünften Erdteils*, Munich, 1959.

Love, J. R. B., 'Rock Paintings of the Worora and their Mythological Interpretation', *Journal of the Royal Society of Western Australia*, 1929-30, xvi, pp. 1-24.

Love, J. R. B., *Stone-age Bushmen of Today*, Glasgow, 1936.

McCarthy, F. D., *Australian Aboriginal Decorative Art*, Sydney, 1958.

McCarthy, F. D., *Australian Aboriginal Rock Art*, Sydney, 1958.

McCarthy, F. D., 'Stencils of the Aborigines', *Australian Museum Magazine*, 1959, xiii, pp. 25-7.

[Martin, J.], *Journals and Reports of Two Voyages to the Glenelg River and the North-West Coast of Australia*, Perth, 1864. Published anonymously.

Mathew, Rev. J., 'The Cave Paintings of Australia, their Authorship and Significance,' *Journal of the Anthropological Institute*, 1894, xxiii, pp. 42-52.

Mountford, C. P., *Aboriginal Paintings—Arnhem Land, Australia*, UNESCO World Art Series No. 3, 1954.

Mountford, C. P., *Records of the American-Australian Scientific Expedition to Arnhem Land*, Melbourne, 1956.

Petri, H., *Sterbende Welt in Nordwestaustralien*, Braunschweig, 1954.

Petri, H., 'Australia', *Encyclopedia of World Art*, 2, pp. 119-123, 126-39.

Playford, P. E., 'Aboriginal Rock Paintings of the West Kimberley Region, Western Australia,' *Journal of the Royal Society of Western Australia*, 1960, 43, pp. 111-22.

Rose, F. G. G., 'An Interpretation of Some Aboriginal Rock Carvings and Paintings in North Western Australia', *Man*, 1950, 13.

Schulz, A., 'North-west Australian Rock Paintings', *Memoir of the National Museum of Victoria*, 1956, pp. 7-57.

Statham, E. J., 'Ancient Script in Australia', *Journal of the Victorian Institute*, 1901, xxxiii, pp. 254-8.

Stokes, J. L., *Discoveries in Australia*, 2 vols, London, 1846.

Willcox, A. R., *The Rock Art of South Africa*, Johannesburg, 1963.

Worsnop, T., *The Prehistoric Arts, Manufactures, Weapons etc. of the Aborigines of Australia*, Adelaide, 1897.

Index

The figures in bold type refer to pages with illustrations

Aboriginal behaviour towards paintings, 9-10, 13, 22, 32
avoidance of touching paintings, 21, 73-4
ceremonies performed near, 37
disregard for Bradshaw figures, 13, 85-6
fear of upsetting spirits, 10 13, 21, 32, 73-4
gifts left at sites, 37, 40
pride in, 13
songs sung near, 33, 37
speeches made to paintings, 9, 26-7, 40, 50, 52
Aboriginal behaviour towards rock engravings, 133-4
Aboriginal behaviour towards tree carvings, 128-9
Admiralty Gulf, 71, **72**, **96**
'Afghan' camel drivers, 96
Agula; see evil spirits
Albert Barunga, 50, 91, 94, 105, 108, 113, 118
Albert Reef, 71
American whaling expeditions, 79
Arndt, W., 28, 30-1
Arnhem Land, **83**, 94, 102
Arunda, 135
Augustus Island, 93-4
Australian Institute of Aboriginal Studies, 13

baler shell painted, 21, **24**, 25
Barnett Range, 111
barramundi, **115**
Barunga; *see* Albert Barunga
Baudin, Nicolas, 61, 78
'Bearded man', **100**, 102
beehive, 117, **117**, 118, 119, **119**
bees, 117, 118
Bigge Island, 58, 72-80
paintings on, **76**, **77**, **78**, 79
Blackfellow Creek, 52

boab trees, 126, 128-31
carvings on, **126-31**
carved nuts from, 131-2, **132**
Bobby Wabi, 10, 73, 133-4
Bonaparte Archipelago, 71
Bradshaw, Joseph, 81
Bradshaw figures, 81-90
paintings of, **81-4**, 86-8, 90
Bramba-bramba, 85
Brimera, 105
Brockman, F. S. and Expedition, **35**, 37, **44**, 45-6, 62, 67, 137
Browse Island, 94
Bundjin-moro, 46-9, **48**
Bundulmeri, 44, 94
Bunggudmana, **48**, 49
burials, **44**, **45**, 46, 56, 94

Calder River, 39, 49
Camden Harbour settlement, 61
Campbell, J., 67
Capell, A., 103
Cape Voltaire, 92
Carlton Hill Station, **23**, 115
Carpenters Gap, 134, **134**, 135
Cassini Island, 61
Chalangdal, 69-70
paintings at, **70**, **74**, **75**
Champagny Island, 94
Charlie Numbulmoore, 50, 98, 107, 123
painting a cave, **24**, 25, **25**, 26, **26**, 27, **27**
child spirits, 33-4, 105-6, **106**, 116
circumcision, 35, 40
Coate, Howard, 13, 18, 64, 68
Cole Creek Station, 107
Collingridge, George, 66-7
creation period, 98-9, 114
crocodile, 101, 119-24
paintings of, **101**, **121**, **123**
tribal marks imitating, 119, **121**

crocodile (*continued*)
tree carving of, **127**
rock engraving of, **135**

Dampier, William, 61, 80
Daualimbi, 106-7, **108**
Daualindi, 55
Derby, 17-18, 60, 131, **131**, **132**
devil-ray, **126**
dingo, 120, 122, **122**
Djandad; see lightning
Djarula, 97
Djibida, 102
Djilgu, 94, **95**, 112, 113, **113**
Djilinga, 134, **134**
Djimi, 91
Djuari, 91, 93, **93**, 94
Doubtful Bay, 18, 56-8, **59**, **100**, 102
Durack River, 50

Eagle Point, 124, **125**
Elkin, A. P., 18, 62, 68, 115
evil spirits, 49, 91, **91**, 92, **92**

fish, 55-7, **59**, 115, 133
fish traps, 37, 56
Fitzroy Crossing, 122
Fitzroy River, 52
flying foxes, 118, **119**
flying squirrels, 118, **120**
Forrest River, 18, 103, 105, **106**, 137
de Freycinet, Louis, 66
Frobenius Expedition, 62

Galaru, 32, 34
Galarungari, 32, 52, 54
Galeru, 103
Geike Gorge, 53
Geological Museum, London, 60
Gibb River, 18, 102-3, 107, 111, 122, 123, 124
paintings near, **109**, **112**, **123**

Glenelg River, 18, 118
  paintings near, **12**, **63**-8, **88**
grasshopper, 85, **85**, 124
Grey, Sir George, 18, 58, 61, 126, 128
  paintings found by, 62, **63**, 64-8, **64**-**8**
Gurangara, 135-6

Halls Point, 54, 93-4
hand stencil, 21, 22, **22**
Heywood Island, 93
House, F. M., 44-6
Hunter River, 113

Inanunga, 39
Indonesian voyaging to Kimberley, 15, 17, 18, 60-1, 66, 94
Indonesian pottery, **19**
Inonga, 120

Jumuru, 44

Kaberry, Phyllis, 34, 105, 115
Kadbung, 111
Kadjingari Island, 72
Kaiara, 44, 69-80, 133
  associated with boats, 76-7; pipes, 74, 76; cyclones, 69-71, 73-4
  Bobby's dream of, 74
  map of routes, **71**
  paintings of, **70**, **72**-9
  similar to Wandjina, 69-70, 73
  speculation on origins of, 76-80
Kakadja, 91, 92, **92**
Kalambi, 98-9
Kalumburu Mission, 17, 45, 70, 85
  paintings near, **82-4**, **90**
Kangaroo painting, **116**
  tree carving, 130
  rock engraving, 136, **136**
Karendjin, 52, 53
Karn-gi, 106-7, **108**, **129**
Karunjie Station
  paintings near, **108**
  tree carvings near, **128-9**
Kimberley Downs, 122
King Leopold Ranges, **11**, 120

King, Philip, 61, 78, 80, 126
King River, 130
Koion, 85
Kubi, 98-9
Kunmunya Mission, 24, 96
  carved boab nuts from, **132**
  carved tree at, **126**
Kuri Bay, 101

lalai, 98
Langgi, 54-61, 79, 80, 137
  ballast stone, **60**
  beach at, **55**
  painting at, **58**
Larawai, 71
Leopold Downs, 101
lightning, 96, **96**, 102
Lily Pool, 101
Linesman's Creek, 135, **135**, 136
lizard, **114**, 124, **125**
Lommel, A., 7, 42, 81, 85-6, 96, 123
Love, Reverend J. R. B., 24, 56-7, 62, 68, 134
Lu, Lumeri, Lumuru, 103, 105

Mamadai, 25-7, 32, 50, **50**, 52
  restoration of painting, **25**, **26**, **27**
Manda, 108-9
Mang-got, 124, **125**
Manning Creek, 44-9, 112, 119-21, 137
  paintings on, **8**, **29**, **44**, **45**, **48**, **91**, **112**, **121**
Martin, James, 61
Meda Station, 122
Meggitt, M. J., 97
Mimi figures, 82, **83**
Miminja, 91-2
moieties, 115
Montague Sound, 71, 73
Montalivet Island, 71, 72
moon, 56, 106, 107, 129, 133
  painting of, **108**
  tree carving of, **129**
Morol, 9, 32, 49-50
Mount Barnett, 53, 133
Mount Barnett Station, 53, 112
Mount Deborah, 32
Mount Elizabeth Station, 81
Mount Hann, 32, 49
Mount Trafalgar, 113

Mount Waterloo, 113
Mudge Bay, 72
Mulu mulu, 65
Munja, 39
Munro, Billy, 120

Namarali, 54-6, **58**
Namri, 118
Napier Range, 17, 18, 33, 120, 122, 134, 135
National Maritime Museum, Greenwich, 79
New Island, 79, 80
Northern Territory, 82, 97
Numbi, 56
Numbulmoore; *see* Charlie Numbulmoore

Oobagooma Station, 120
Oscar Range, 17, 18, 51-2, 120
  paintings in, **51**
Ord River, 15, 103, 136, 138
  paintings on, **13**, **17**, **114**, **115**, **116**
  rock engravings on, **136**

painting techniques, 21-7
  illustrations of, **22-7**
paintings
  ceremonies associated with, 13, 33, 37
  conservation of, 137-9
  damaged by water, 137-8
  dates, 57, 89-90, 118
  locations, 18, 20
  restoration, 21, 25-7, 37, 57
  superimpositions, 57-8
Panton, J., 66
Parry Harbour, 105
Peron, François, 66
Penrose, Ray, 17, 28
Pentacost Range, 131, **131**
Perulba, 113, 118-9
  paintings at, **119**, **120**
Petri, H., 35-6
Filbara region, 133, 135-6
Pindjauri, **51**, 52
polished stones, 103, 108, 112
Port Keats, 94
Playford, P., 120
Plenderleith, H. J., 139
Prince Frederick Harbour, **104**, **110**

Prince Regent River, 49, 57, 105, 112-13, 118-19; see also Perulba
Prudhoe Island, 71, 133, **133**, 134, **134**

Queensland, 82

rituals associated with paintings, 35-7, 43
ritual killing; see ulu
rock engravings, 46, 96, 97, 133-6
    illustrations of, **47**, **95**, **97**, **133-6**
Roger Strait, 79, 80

St George Basin, 101, **111**, 112; see also Djilgu
Sam Woolagoodjah, 13, **20**, 22, **22**, **24**, 25, 49, 54-6, 65, 102, 118, 119, **121**, 124
Scheepvaart Museum, Amsterdam, 79
Schulz, Agnes, 81
Scott Strait, 78
Secure Bay, 18, 22, 117, **117**, 118
Sholl, H., 61
Sidie, 54, 60, **61**
snakes, 103-13, 128-30
    paintings of, **104**, **108**, **109**, **112**, **113**
    tree carvings of, **128**, **129**
stingray, 118, **120**

Stokes, J. Lort, 61, 79, 80
stone arrangements, 42, 43, **43**, 46, **47**, 53, 72
Strehlow, T. G. H., 135
Sturt Creek Station, 96, 97, 133
    rock engravings at, **97**
subincision, 35, 40
Sunday Island, 132

Tasman, Abel, 60, 77-8
Thornton, S., 67
totems, 115-17, 124
Tumbi, 39
Tunbai, 31-2, 38-40, 42-3, 44, 46, 49, 54
    illustrations of, **38**, **39**, **43**
turtles, **136**

ulu, 107, 109, **110**, 111, 122
Ungamin, 94, **95**
Ungud; see snakes
Unmeleri, 119-20, **121**

Vansittart Bay, 70, 88, 111

Wabi; see Bobby Wabi
Wadanda, 52, **52**, 53, **53**
Walamut, 41, **42**
Walbiri, 97
Wanalirri, **14**, 40, 41, **41**, 42, **42**, 45, 54
Wandjinas
    and fertility, 33-4

Wandjinas (continued)
    and storms, 28, 30-3, 50, 52
    behaviour of, 35-6, 42, 46, 65
Wandjina paintings, 8, **14**, 24-7, **29**, **30**, 35-6, **41-2**, **44-5**, **48**, **50-1**, **53**, **58-9**, **63**, **66-8**, **109**, **113**
    and ulu figures, 109, 111
    ceremonies at, 37
    gifts left at, 37, 40
Wandjina rock engraving, **52**
Waningga, 118
Warabi, 71, **73**
Warangala, 72
Warner, W. L., 94
Warulu, 94, **95**
Western Australian Museum, 132
Widjaru, 44
Willcox, A. R., 81
Windjina Gorge, 33, 122
Wodjin, 31, 38-40, 41, **41**, 54
Woolagoodjah; see Sam Woolagoodjah
Worms, Father E. A., 135-6
Worora, 103
Worsnop, Thomas, 66
Wunambal, 103
Wunduk, 123-4
Wurwai, 71, **72**
Wyndham, 15, 128, 130-2
    carved boab nuts from, **132**
    carved tree at, **127**, 130
    painting at, **93**

X-ray painting, 102

yams, 94, 99, **99**, 101